ECLECTIC E

SHAKESPEARE'S

HAMLET

EDITED BY

ALBERT E. SHOWER, B. A.

ENGLISH DEPARTMENT, BURLINGTON HIGH SCHOOL
BURLINGTON, IOWA

NEW YORK ∴ CINCINNATI ∴ CHICAGO
AMERICAN BOOK COMPANY

INTRODUCTION.

SEVERAL quarto editions of Shakespeare's tragedy of "Hamlet, Prince of Denmark," were in print previous to its appearance in the famous folio of 1623, — the first published collection of the poet's dramas, and the edition to which modern editors generally look for the genuine text of his plays. Of these quartos, that of 1604 is regarded as authentic, and a useful auxiliary in throwing light on obscure passages in the "Hamlet" text of the folio.

The story on which the tragedy is founded is told by Saxo Grammaticus in his "Historia Danica," written in Latin about the end of the twelfth century. It is included in Belleforest's "Histoires Tragiques," published in Paris in 1570. The first English translation we have of the story appeared in 1608, under the title of "The Hystorie of Hamblet," although it is possible there was an earlier English edition.

Shakespeare, however, owes but little to the original story, whatever the shape in which it came to him. He found in the records of a barbarous period a tale of conjugal infelicity, murder, and revenge, together with some rude indication of the character of Hamlet. " But," as Knight observes, " what he has given us is so essentially a creation, from first to last, that it would be only tedious to point out the lesser resemblances between the drama

and the history." The period of the action of the play is the
same as that of the relation by the Danish historian,—a period
anterior to the Norman Conquest, when England was either under
the sovereignty of the Northmen, or paid tribute to the Danish
power.

It has been justly remarked that "'Hamlet' is not Shakespeare's greatest play, nor does it contain his greatest poetry."
Yet it has probably contributed more to his fame than any other
one production of his genius. It has been translated into all the
languages of Europe, and has engaged the attention, and won
the admiration, of the most eminent scholars, philosophers, and
poets, not only among those

> "—— who speak the tongue
> That Shakespeare spake,"

but throughout the civilized world; and the commentaries on the
nature and action of the drama generally, and of the character of
Hamlet especially, are innumerable. We have not far to look for
the reason of the continued and unabated popularity of "Hamlet," and our perennial interest in its title character. As Hazlitt
aptly says, "It is the one of Shakespeare's plays we think of the
oftenest, because it abounds in striking reflections of human life,
and because the distresses of Hamlet are transferred, by the turn
of his mind, to the general account of humanity. . . . Whatever
happens to him we apply to ourselves, because he applies it so
himself, as a means of general reasoning. He is a great moral-
izer; and what makes him worth attending to is, that he moralizes
on his own feelings and experience. . . . His speeches and
sayings are as real as our own thoughts. Their reality is in the
reader's mind. It is *we* who are Hamlet."

The opening scene of the tragedy is at Elsinore, in front of the castle of the Danish King, where, as it is rumored, the night watch has seen on two occasions a Ghost resembling Hamlet, the lately deceased King. Horatio, a friend of the young Prince Hamlet, while he has little faith in the rumor, has, at the solicitation of the sentinels, consented to share the watch with them, that he may see and speak to the Apparition, should it present itself. Twice before the dawn, the Ghost appears. Horatio addresses it, but receives no reply, though on its second appearance it lifted its head as about to speak, when, at the crowing of the morning cock, it faded away. Horatio, now convinced that the Ghost is no illusion, predicts that its appearance bodes some evil to the State; and it is agreed that he, with his companions, shall visit young Hamlet, and communicate to him what they have seen.

The next scene is a room in the castle, where Claudius the King, Gertrude the Queen, Hamlet her son, Polonius an old chamberlain, his son Laertes, and others, are assembled. Here we learn from the King that he succeeded to the throne on the death of his brother, whose widow he has married; that an invasion of the kingdom is threatened by young Fortinbras, Prince of Norway; that he is about to send ambassadors to the King of that country, the uncle of the Prince, to remonstrate against the warlike preparations of the nephew. He then grants Laertes' request to return to Paris, whence he had come to attend the King's coronation; then, turning to Hamlet, Claudius and the Queen expostulate with him on his excessive and continued grief for his father's death, and urge him to give up all thought of his proposed return to the college at Wittenberg. Hamlet yields to his mother's wishes, but presently, when left alone, expresses his contempt and hatred of the King, and his horror at the unseemly and unnatural marriage of his mother, so quickly following his father's death, and with a brother of her former husband. While he is soliloquizing, Horatio, with Marcellus and Bernardo, the officers of the guard, enter, and recount to him the occurrences of the previous night. Satisfied from their description that it is his father's spirit they have seen, he determines to watch with them, that he may learn, if possible, the cause and object of the mysterious visitation.

In the third scene, Laertes, taking leave of his sister Ophelia, cautions her to fear the wooing of Hamlet, who has professed love for her. Polonius, coming in, gives his blessing and some good advice to his son, and when he goes out the old chamberlain also bids his daughter be wary of the attentions of the young Prince.

The fourth scene is, as before, at midnight, on the platform in front of the castle. Here, according to appointment, Hamlet has joined Horatio and Marcellus in the watch for the Apparition. While Hamlet is commenting on the disgraceful orgies with which his mother's wedding is celebrated, the Ghost makes its appearance. Hamlet speaks to it, conjures it to tell the reason of its coming, and what it would the living should do. The Apparition makes no answer, but beckons Hamlet to follow, which he does; and, when out of the hearing of his companions, the Ghost makes known that he is the Spirit of Hamlet's father; that his death was not occasioned by the sting of a serpent, as had been reported, but that he was poisoned, while sleeping in his garden, by his brother, who now wears his crown, and has wedded his widowed queen. Then, charging Hamlet to avenge his father's murder on his perfidious uncle, the Ghost vanishes as it "scents the morning air."

Horatio and Marcellus, fearing some harm to Hamlet, are hastening to seek him, when he meets them, and in answer to their inquiries speaks at first jestingly of his interview with the Ghost, but afterwards causes them to swear that they will reveal nothing of the events of the night, nor indicate by any word or gesture, however odd or strange his act or speech should hereafter be, that they could, if they would, give a reason for his conduct. The solemnity of the oath is increased by the voice of the Ghost beneath calling on them to swear.

At the opening of the second act we are at Polonius' house, where he is dispatching Reynaldo, his servant, to Paris, to learn something of Laertes' way of living in that city. As he goes out, Ophelia enters in great alarm to inform her father that, while she was sewing in her room, Hamlet came in, — staring wildly, his dress disordered, and apparently out of his mind, — and seizing her by the wrist gazed steadfastly on her face for a time, then, dropping her hand, left her presence, with his eyes fixed on her to the last. After questioning his daughter, and learning that she had obeyed his injunction, and treated Hamlet coldly, — returning his letters, and refusing to see him, — Polonius concludes that this rejection of his love by Ophelia has made Hamlet mad, and determines to so advise the King and Queen, who had noticed, and were much disturbed by, his eccentric behavior.

In the second scene of this act we meet Rosencrantz and Guildenstern, two friends of Hamlet. They have been sent for by the King, in the hope that in free intercourse with Hamlet, without arousing his suspicion that they are acting on the King's prompting, they may get from him the cause of his distraction. Polonius, now coming in, announces the return of the ambassadors from Norway, and also that he has discovered the cause of Hamlet's lunacy. The ambassadors having been heard, Polonius proceeds, with many words and in an inflated style, to inform the King and Queen that it is his daughter's rejection of Hamlet's addresses that has made him mad. To satisfy the King that such is the case, Polonius proposes that the King conceal himself where he can overhear a conversation between Hamlet and Ophelia, — an arrangement of which she is to be advised. The King and Queen go out. Hamlet enters; and his discordant talk with Polonius confirms his opinion of the cause of Hamlet's disordered mind.

Rosencrantz and Guildenstern come in; but, instead of probing Hamlet's madness, they are completely outwitted by him. He is interested, however, when they tell him of a company of players that is just now about the court; and he determines in his own mind to have a play enacted before the King and Queen, in which he will insert some lines describing a scene like the murder of his father, while he himself will watch the effect of the performance on the King. The act closes with a soliloquy by Hamlet, wherein he blames himself for his delay in executing his vengeance, expresses doubt of the truth of the Ghost's revelation, but concludes, that, if the King is guilty, the play will test his guilt beyond question.

The third act begins with the relation by Rosencrantz and Guildenstern of their visit to Hamlet. Then comes the meeting between Hamlet and Ophelia, as planned by her father. The King, who, as contemplated, has been a hidden listener, does not think that Hamlet's speech and actions are occasioned by love, nor does he deem them altogether due to madness. His guilty conscience is quick to apprehend some danger to himself; and he resolves that Hamlet shall be sent to England without delay, intending that he shall there be put to death.

The next scene embraces the play before the King and Court.

which comes so near the circumstances of the murder as related by the Ghost, that the King rises, and leaves the hall, followed by all in attendance except Hamlet and Horatio. Rosencrantz and Guildenstern soon reënter with a message to Hamlet from his mother, who desires to speak with him in her chamber. He complies with her request, and in an interview, casting aside all disguise of madness, reproaches her in bitter terms for her disloyalty to his father in her hasty and unnatural marriage with the brother and murderer of her former husband. Affrighted by the violence of his speech, she calls for help. The cry is repeated by Polonius, who is concealed behind the drapery of the room, through which Hamlet pierces with his rapier (supposing the eavesdropper to be the King), and kills the unseen old man. Overcome by the earnestness of her son's appeals, the Queen displays contrition, promises repentance, and further promises that she will not make known to the King the fact that Hamlet's apparent madness is assumed.

In the fourth act the Queen reports to the King that Hamlet *in a fit of madness* has killed Polonius. The King sends for Hamlet, tells him that his safety requires that he should leave the country, and that the vessel is ready to take him to England. Following Hamlet's departure there is a scene in which Ophelia appears in disheveled dress, singing bits of old ballads, her mind distracted by grief for the death of her father.

Laertes now arrives from Paris, in hot haste to avenge his father's murder. He at first thinks the King accessory to the deed, but is soon convinced, after meeting him, that he is also an object of Hamlet's enmity. While the King and Laertes are in conference, messengers come in, bringing letters from Hamlet, from which we gather that he has been captured by pirates, and by them landed, naked and alone, on the shore of Denmark, and that he intends to come to Elsinore at once. Whereupon the King contrives a plan to take Hamlet's life on his return to court. The King is to have Hamlet and Laertes engage in a friendly fencing match, in which Laertes is to kill Hamlet by using, as if inadvertently, a foil without a blunted point. To this Laertes readily agrees, and adds that he will have his weapon's point so envenomed with a deadly poison that the merest scratch with it will be mortal; and, to make all sure, the King is to prepare a cup of poisoned wine, of which Hamlet may be induced to drink between the heats of the contest. Hardly are the details of this plot completed, when the Queen enters with the news of the accidental drowning of Ophelia.

The fifth act opens in a graveyard, where Hamlet, who has just reached Elsinore, is moralizing over a skull which the gravedigger has thrown out with the earth while digging a grave. The King, the Queen, Laertes, and other mourners approach in funeral procession, following the body of Ophelia. At the burial, a violent quarrel arises between Hamlet and Laertes; but they are finally reconciled.

The fencing match takes place the next day. In one of the bouts, Hamlet receives a slight wound from Laertes' poisoned foil, and the fencers become incensed. In the excitement there is an exchange of weapons, and Laertes is punctured with his own deadly instrument. In the meantime the Queen, who is ignorant of the poisoned cup, drinks of it, and immediately falls dead. Laertes now tells Hamlet that neither he nor himself have half an hour to live, and confesses the treacherous plot devised by himself and the King; hearing which, Hamlet rushes upon the King, and stabs him to death.

The play ends with the arrival of Fortinbras, who claims some rights in the kingdom; and, with Hamlet's dying voice in his favor, he succeeds by election to the Danish crown.

Professor Dowden ("Shakespeare, his Plays and Poems"), in his remarks on "Hamlet," observes, "No play of Shakespeare's has had a higher power of interesting spectators and readers, and none has given rise to a greater variety of conflicting interpretations. It has been rightly named a tragedy of thought; and in this respect, as well as others, takes its place beside 'Julius Cæsar.' Neither Brutus nor Hamlet is the victim of an over-mastering passion, as are the chief persons of the later tragedies; e.g., Othello, Macbeth, Coriolanus. The burden of a terrible duty is laid upon each of them, and neither is fitted for bearing such a burden. Brutus is disqualified for action by his moral idealism, his student-like habits, his capacity for dealing with abstractions rather than with men and things. Hamlet is disqualified for action by his excess of the reflective tendency and by his unstable will, which alternates between complete inactivity and fits of excited energy. Naturally sensitive, he receives a painful shock from the hasty second marriage of his mother; already the springs of faith and joy in his nature are imbittered; then follows the terrible discovery of his father's murder, with the injunction laid upon him to revenge the crime; upon this again follow the repulses which he receives from Ophelia. A deep melancholy lays hold of his spirit, and all of his life grows dark and sad to his vision. Although hating his father's murderer, he has little heart to push on his revenge. He is aware that he is suspected, and surrounded by spies. Partly to baffle them, partly to create a veil behind which to seclude his true self, partly because his whole moral nature is indeed deeply disordered, he assumes the part of one whose wits have gone astray. Except for one loyal friend, he is alone among enemies or supposed traitors. Ophelia he regards as no more loyal or honest to him than his mother had been to her dead husband. The ascertainment of Claudius' guilt by means of the play still leaves him incapable of the last decisive act of vengeance. Not so, however, with the King, who, now recognizing his foe in Hamlet, does not delay to dispatch him to a bloody death in England. But there is in Hamlet a terrible power of sudden and desperate action. From the melancholy which broods over him after the burial of Ophelia, he rouses himself to the play of swords with Laertes, and at the last, with strength which leaps up before its final extinction, he accomplishes the punishment of the malefactor.

". Horatio, with his fortitude, his self-possession, his strong equanimity, is a contrast to the Prince. And Laertes, who takes violent measures at the shortest notice to revenge *his* father's murder, is in another way a contrast. But Laertes is the young gallant of the period; and his capacity for action arises in part from the absence of those moral checks of which Hamlet is sensible. Polonius is owner of the shallow wisdom of this world, and exhibits this grotesquely while now on the brink of dotage: he sees, but cannot see through, Hamlet's ironical mockery of him. Ophelia is tender, affectionate, but the reverse of heroic. She fails Hamlet in his need, and then, in her turn becoming the sufferer, gives way under the pressure of her afflictions."

Hazlitt ("Characters of Shakespeare's Plays," London, 1869), in a critical notice of this play, remarks, "If 'Lear' is distinguished by the greatest depth of passion, 'Hamlet' is the most

remarkable for the ingenuity, originality, and unstudied development of character. Shakespeare had more magnanimity than
any other poet, and he has shown more of it in this play than in
any other. There is no attempt to force an interest: everything
is left for time and circumstances to unfold. The attention is
excited without effort, the incidents succeed each other as matters
of course, the characters think and speak and act just as they
might do if left entirely to themselves. There is no set purpose,
no straining at a point. The observations are suggested by the
passing scene. . . . The whole play is an exact transcript of
what might be supposed to have taken place at the court of
Denmark, at the remote period of time fixed upon, before the
modern refinements in morals and manners were heard of. . . .

"The character of Hamlet stands quite by itself. It is not a
character marked by strength of will or even of passion, but by
refinement of thought and sentiment. Hamlet is as little of the
hero as a man can well be; but he is a young and princely novice,
full of high enthusiasm and quick sensibility,—the sport of circumstances, questioning with fortune, and refining on his own
feelings, and forced from the natural bias of his disposition by
the strangeness of his situation. He seems incapable of deliberate action, and is only hurried into extremities on the spur of the
occasion, when he has no time to reflect, as in the scene where
he kills Polonius, and again, where he alters the letters which
Rosencrantz and Guildenstern are taking with them to England,
purporting his death. At other times, when he is most bound to
act, he remains puzzled, undecided, and skeptical, dallies with his
purposes till the occasion is lost, and finds out some pretense to
relapse into indolence and thoughtfulness again. For this reason
he refuses to kill the King when he is at his prayers, and by a

refinement in malice, which is in truth only an excuse for his own
want of resolution, defers his revenge to a more fatal opportunity, when he shall be engaged in 'some act that has no relish
of salvation in't.' . . .

"He is the prince of philosophical speculators; and because he
cannot have his revenge perfect . . . he declines it altogether. So
he scruples to trust the suggestions of the Ghost, contrives the scene
of the play to have surer proof of his uncle's guilt, and then rests
satisfied with this confirmation of his suspicions and the success
of his experiment, instead of acting upon it. Yet he is sensible
of his own weakness, taxes himself with it, and tries to reason
himself out of it. . . . It is not from any want of attachment
to his father, or of abhorrence of his murder, that Hamlet is thus
dilatory; but it is more to his taste to indulge his imagination in
reflecting upon the enormity of the crime, and refining on his
schemes of vengeance, than to put them into immediate practice.
His ruling passion is to think, not to act; and any vague pretext
that flatters this propensity instantly diverts him from his previous purposes. . . .

"Nothing can be more affecting or beautiful than the Queen's
apostrophe to Ophelia on throwing the flowers into the grave.
Shakespeare was thoroughly a master of the mixed motives of
human character, and he here shows us the Queen, who was so
criminal in some respects, not without sensibility and affection
in other relations of life. Ophelia is a character almost too
exquisitely touching to be dwelt upon. 'O rose of May!' O
flower too soon faded! Her love, her madness, her death, are
described with the truest touches of tenderness and pathos. It
is a character which nobody but Shakespeare could have drawn
in the way that he has done, and to the conception of which

there is not even the smallest approach, except in some of the old romantic ballads. Her brother, Laertes, is a character we do not like so well: he is too hot and choleric, and somewhat rodomontade. Polonius is a perfect character in its kind; nor is there any foundation for the objections which have been made to the consistency of this part. It is said that he acts very foolishly, and talks very sensibly. There is no inconsistency in that. Again: that he talks wisely at one time, and foolishly at another; that his advice to Laertes is very excellent, and his advice to the King and Queen on the subject of Hamlet's madness very ridiculous. But he gives the one as a father, and is sincere in it: he gives the other as a mere courtier, a busybody, and is accordingly officious, garrulous, and impertinent. In short, Shakespeare has been accused of inconsistency in this and other characters, only because he has kept up the distinction which there is in nature between the understandings and the moral habits of men ; between the . . . [wisdom] of their ideas and the absurdity of their motives. Polonius is not a fool, but he makes himself so. His folly, whether in his actions or speeches, comes under the head of impropriety of intention."

"It has often been remarked," says Rev. Charles E. Moberly (Introduction to "Hamlet"), "how admirably the subordinate characters of this play contrast with and support the grand central one of Hamlet. Ophelia is no Portia, fit to cope with men in argument. Her character is one of repose, — just the one in which the dialectic and generalizing spirit of Hamlet would meet its due opposite. She is full of simple religion, even in her madness; while he is at the best skeptical and vague in his thoughts on this subject. . . . In like manner, Horatio stands in the directest contrast to Hamlet.   He is the 'pruner of his periods,' the controller of his flights of imagination, the protester against extravagances of speech.   He is also opposed to him as being the man on whose composure good or bad fortune has no influence; the man so faithful to himself that he can never be false to any other man.   But above all other contrasts in the play stands out that which Hamlet himself recognizes,— the one between himself and Laertes.   The latter is as purely worldly in his thoughts as Hamlet is the reverse.   He is the man of Parisian training.   Fencing and music are his studies.   He is false and treacherous, as one trained at the court of France in Shakespeare's time was likely to be; while Hamlet is most generous, and void of suspicion.   In all his utterances there is no tinge of Hamlet's reflectiveness.   But in spite of all this there is one quality in which he is immeasurably Hamlet's superior.   This is that important one of instant energy and decision.   When his father is slain, he does exactly what Hamlet longs in vain to be able to do,— he 'sweeps' home from France to his revenge.   Nor is any needless moment of time allowed to pass before he is bursting open the gates of the palace, with a crowd of partisans at his back who are already proclaiming him King of Denmark,— a more apt one, perhaps, for those rough days, than poor Hamlet would have been."

The following remarks on Ophelia are selected from Mrs. Jameson's delineation of the character ("Characteristics of Women," Boston, 1875): "Beyond every character that Shakespeare has drawn (Hamlet alone excepted), that of Ophelia makes us forget the poet in his own creation.   Whenever we bring her to mind, it is with the same exclusive sense of her real existence, without reference to the wondrous power which called her into life. The effect (and what an effect!) is produced by means so simple, by strokes so few and so unobtrusive, that we take no thought of them. It is so purely natural and unsophisticated, yet so profound in its pathos, that, as Hazlitt observes, it takes us back to the old ballads: we forget that in its perfect artlessness it is the supreme and consummate triumph of art. . . . It is the helplessness of Ophelia, arising merely from her innocence, and pictured without any indication of weakness, which melts us with such profound pity. She is so young, that neither her mind nor her person has attained maturity. She is not aware of the nature of her own feelings: they are prematurely developed in their full force before she has strength to bear them; and love and grief together rend and shatter the frail texture of her existence, like the burning fluid poured into a crystal vase. She says very little, and what she does say seems rather intended to hide than to reveal the emotions of her heart; yet in those few words we are made as perfectly acquainted with her character, and with what is passing in her mind, as if she had thrown forth her soul with all the glowing eloquence of Juliet. . . . When her father catechises her . . . he extorts from her in short sentences, uttered with bashful reluctance, the confession of Hamlet's love for her, but not a word of her love for him. The whole scene is managed with inexpressible delicacy. It is one of those instances, common in Shakespeare, in which we are allowed to perceive what is passing in the mind of a person without any consciousness on his part. Only Ophelia herself is unaware, that, while she is admitting the extent of Hamlet's courtship, she is also betraying how deep is the impression it has made, how entire the love with which it is returned. . . . Of her subsequent madness, what can be said ?   What an affecting, what an astonishing, picture of a mind utterly, hopelessly wrecked ! — past hope, past cure !   There is the frenzy of excited passion; there is the madness caused by intense and continued thought; there is the delirium of fevered nerves. But Ophelia's madness is distinct from these; it is not the suspension, but the utter destruction, of the reasoning powers; it is the total imbecility which, as medical people well know, frequently follows some terrible shock to the spirits.   Constance is frantic; Lear is mad; Ophelia is *insane.*   Her sweet mind lies in fragments before us — a pitiful spectacle !   Her wild, rambling fancies; her aimless, broken speeches; her quick transitions from gayety to sadness, — each equally purposeless and causeless; her snatches of old ballads, such as perhaps her nurse sung her to sleep with in her infancy, — are all so true to life that we forget to wonder, and can only weep.   It belonged to Shakespeare alone so to temper such a picture that we can endure to dwell upon it.

> " Thought and affliction, passion, hell itself,
>   She turns to favor and to prettiness."

Exponent of Modern Drama

Henrick Ibsen (Sweden).

30, 17, 80, 7, 6, 3, 1

HAMLET, PRINCE OF DENMARK.

PERSONS OF THE PLAY.

CLAUDIUS, King of Denmark.
HAMLET, *son to the late, and nephew to the present King.*
POLONIUS, *lord chamberlain.*
HORATIO, *friend to Hamlet.*
LAERTES, *son to Polonius.*
VOLTIMAND,
CORNELIUS,
ROSENCRANTZ,
GUILDENSTERN, } *courtiers.*
OSRIC,
A Gentleman,
A Priest.
MARCELLUS, } *officers.*
BERNARDO,
FRANCISCO, *a soldier.*

REYNALDO, *servant to Polonius.*
Players.
Two Clowns, *gravediggers.*
FORTINBRAS, Prince of Norway.
A Captain.
English Ambassadors.

GERTRUDE, Queen of Denmark, *mother to Hamlet.*
OPHELIA, *daughter to Polonius.*

Lords, Ladies, Officers, Soldiers, Sailors, Messengers, and other Attendants.

Ghost of Hamlet's Father.

SCENE: *Denmark.*

ACT I.

SCENE I. *Elsinore. A Platform before the Castle.*

FRANCISCO *at his post. Enter to him* BERNARDO.

Bernardo. Who's there?
Francisco. Nay, answer me:[1] stand, and unfold yourself.
Bernardo. Long live the King!

[1] " Me " is here used with emphasis. It is for the sentinel on duty to challenge all comers, and demand the watchword; which here Bernardo immediately gives.

Francisco. Bernardo?

Bernardo. He.

Francisco. You come most carefully upon your hour.

Bernardo. 'Tis now struck twelve: get thee to bed, Francisco.

Francisco. For this relief much thanks: 'tis bitter cold,
And I am sick at heart.

Bernardo. Have you had quiet guard?

Francisco.   Not a mouse stirring.

Bernardo. Well, good night.
If you do meet Horatio and Marcellus,
The rivals [1] of my watch, bid them make haste.

Francisco. I think I hear them.—Stand, ho!   Who's there?

Enter HORATIO *and* MARCELLUS.

Horatio. Friends to this ground.

Marcellus.   And liegemen to the Dane.[2]

Francisco. Give you good night.

Marcellus.   O, farewell, honest soldier:
Who hath reliev'd you?

Francisco.   Bernardo has my place.
Give you good night.   [*Exit.*

Marcellus.   Holla! Bernardo!

Bernardo.   Say,
What, is Horatio there?

Horatio.   A piece of him.

Bernardo. Welcome, Horatio: welcome, good Marcellus.

Marcellus. What, has this thing appear'd again to-night?

Bernardo. I have seen nothing.

Marcellus. Horatio says 'tis but our fantasy,[3]
And will not let belief take hold of him
Touching this dreaded sight, twice seen of us:
Therefore I have entreated him along

---

[1] Partners.

[2] "Liegemen to the Dane," i.e., subjects of the King of Denmark.

[3] Fancy; imagination.

With us to watch the minutes of this night;
That if again this apparition come,
He may approve [1] our eyes, and speak to it.

   Horatio. Tush, tush, 'twill not appear.

   Bernardo.   Sit down a while;
And let us once again assail your ears,
That are so fortified against our story,
What we have two nights seen.

   Horatio.   Well, sit we down,
And let us hear Bernardo speak of this.

   Bernardo. Last night of all,
When yond same star that's westward from the pole
Had made his course to illume that part of heaven
Where now it burns, Marcellus and myself,
The bell then beating one, —

Enter GHOST.

   Marcellus. Peace, break thee off: look, where it comes
      again!

   Bernardo. In the same figure, like the King that's dead.

   Marcellus. Thou art a scholar; [2] speak to it, Horatio.

   Bernardo. Looks it not like the King? mark it, Horatio.

   Horatio. Most like: it harrows me with fear and wonder.

   Bernardo. It would be spoke to.

   Marcellus.   Question it, Horatio.

   Horatio. What art thou that usurp'st this time of night,
Together with that fair and warlike form
In which the Majesty of buried Denmark
Did sometimes [3] march? by Heaven I charge thee, speak!

   Marcellus. It is offended.

[1] Corroborate.

[2] Exorcisms (ceremonies for the expulsion of evil spirits) were performed
in Latin, therefore only by scholars: hence the popular belief that they alone
could converse with supernatural apparitions.

[3] Some time; formerly.

Bernardo.   See, it stalks away !

Horatio. Stay ! speak, speak !   I charge thee, speak !

[*Exit Ghost.*

Marcellus. 'Tis gone, and will not answer.

Bernardo. How now, Horatio ! you tremble and look pale.
Is not this something more than fantasy ?
What think you on't ?

Horatio. Before my God, I might not this believe
Without the sensible and true avouch [1]
Of mine own eyes.

Marcellus.   Is it not like the King ?

Horatio. As thou art to thyself.
Such was the very armor he had on
When he the ambitious Norway [2] combated ;
So frown'd he once, when, in an angry parle, [3]
He smote the sledded Polacks [4] on the ice.
'Tis strange.

Marcellus. Thus twice before, and jump [5] at this dead hour,
With martial stalk [6] hath he gone by our watch.

Horatio. In what particular thought to work I know not ;
But in the gross and scope of my opinion, [7]
This bodes some strange eruption to our State.

Marcellus. Good now, sit down, and tell me, he that knows,
Why this same strict and most observant watch
So nightly toils the subject [8] of the land ;
And why such daily cast of brazen cannon,
And foreign mart [9] for implements of war ;
Why such impress [10] of shipwrights, whose sore task
Does not divide the Sunday from the week ;

---

[1] Evidence.   [2] Norwegian King.   [3] Parley or debate.
[4] Inhabitants of Póland ; Polanders.
[5] Just.   [6] Step.
[7] " In what particular thought," etc., i.e., I do not know what particular
train of thought to follow ; but the general tendency of my opinion is that, etc.
[8] Subjects.   [9] Market.   [10] Impressment.

What might be toward,[1] that this sweaty haste
Doth make the night joint laborer with the day:
Who is't that can inform me?

   Horatio.   That can I;
At least, the whisper goes so.   Our last King,
Whose image even but now appear'd to us,
Was, as you know, by Fortinbras of Norway,
Thereto prick'd on by a most emulate[2] pride,
Dar'd to the combat; in which our valiant Hamlet——
For so this side of our known world esteem'd him——
Did slay this Fortinbras; who, by a seal'd compact',
Well ratified by law and heraldry,
Did forfeit with his life all those his lands
Which he stood seiz'd of,[3] to the conqueror:
Against the which, a moiety competent[4]
Was gaged by our King; which had return'd
To the inheritance of Fortinbras,
Had he been vanquisher; as, by the same cov'nant,
And carriage of the article design'd,
His fell to Hamlet. Now, sir, young Fortinbras,
Of unimproved mettle[5] hot and full,
Hath in the skirts of Norway, here and there,
Shark'd up[6] a list of lawless resolutes,
For food and diet, to some enterprise
That hath a stomach in't;[7] which is no other——
As it doth well appear unto our State——

    1 Coming on.

    2 Emulous.

    3 "Seiz'd of," i.e., possessed of; a legal phrase applying to land.   It is still in use.

    4 "Moiety competent," i.e., an adequate portion.

    5 Dr. Johnson notes, that "'full of unimproved mettle' is full of spirit not regulated or guided by experience."

    6 "Shark'd up," i.e., collected indiscriminately.

    7 "Some enterprise," etc., i.e., "some undertaking requiring courage [stomach] in those that attempt it."

But to recover of us, by strong hand
And terms compulsative,[1] those foresaid lands
So by his father lost.   And this, I take it,
Is the main motive of our preparations,
The source of this our watch, and the chief head
Of this posthaste and romage [2] in the land.

Bernardo. I think it be no other but e'en so:
Well may it sort that this portentous figure
Comes armed through our watch; so like the King
That was and is the question of these wars.

Horatio. A mote it is to trouble the mind's eye.
In the most high and palmy state of Rome,
A little ere the mightiest Julius fell,
The graves stood tenantless and the sheeted dead
Did squeak and gibber in the Roman streets:
As stars [3] with trains of fire and dews of blood,
Disasters in the sun; and the moist star [4]
Upon whose influence [5] Neptune's [6] empire stands
Was sick almost to doomsday with eclipse:
And even the like precurse [7] of fierce events,
As harbingers preceding still the fates,
And prologue to the omen coming on,
Have heaven and earth together demonstrated
Unto our climatures [8] and countrymen. —
But soft, behold ! lo, where it comes again !

[1] Compulsatory.

[2] Tumultuous hurry.

[3] A line has probably dropped out of the text preceding these words: " As stars," etc.   That there is a break in it here is evident.

[4] The moon.

[5] Referring to the ebb and flow of the tides.

[6] " When Jupiter assigned to each of his brothers a separate portion of the universe, he decreed that Neptune . . . should be sole monarch of the ocean." — GUERBER: *Myths of Greece and Rome*, p. 149.

[7] Foreshadowing.

[8] Land; country.

Reënter GHOST.

I'll cross it, though it blast me.[1]—Stay, illusion!
If thou hast any sound, or use of voice,
Speak to me:
If there be any good thing to be done,
That may to thee do ease, and grace to me,
Speak to me: [*Cock crows.*
If thou art privy to thy country's fate,
Which, happily, foreknowing may avoid,
O, speak!
Or if thou hast uphoarded in thy life
Extorted treasure in the womb of earth,
For which, they say, you spirits oft walk in death,
Speak of it: stay, and speak!—Stop it, Marcellus.

 Marcellus. Shall I strike it with my partisan?[2]
 Horatio. Do, if it will not stand.
 Bernardo.   'Tis here!
 Horatio.   'Tis here!
 Marcellus. 'Tis gone!   [*Exit Ghost.*

We do it wrong, being so majestical,
To offer it the show of violence;
For it is, as the air, invulnerable,
And our vain blows malicious mockery.

 Bernardo. It was about to speak when the cock crew.
 Horatio. And then it started like a guilty thing
Upon a fearful summons. I have heard,
The cock, that is the trumpet to the morn,
Doth with his lofty and shrill-sounding throat
Awake the god of day; and at his warning,
Whether in sea or fire, in earth or air,
Th' extravagant and erring[3] spirit hies

---

 [1] It was an old superstition, that whoever crossed the spot on which a specter was seen became subject to its malignant influence.

 [2] A weapon resembling a long-handled ax; a halberd.

 [3] "Extravagant and erring," i.e., roving and wandering.

To his confine': and of the truth herein
This present object made probation.[1]

   Marcellus. It faded on the crowing of the cock.
Some say that ever 'gainst that season comes
Wherein our Saviour's birth is celebrated,
The bird of dawning singeth all night long:
And then, they say, no spirit dare stir abroad;
The nights are wholesome; then no planets strike,[2]
No fairy takes,[3] nor witch hath power to charm,
So hallow'd and so gracious is the time.

   Horatio. So have I heard, and do in part believe it.
But look, the morn, in russet mantle clad,
Walks o'er the dew of yon high eastern hill.
Break we our watch up; and by my advice,
Let us impart what we have seen to-night
Unto young Hamlet; for, upon my life,
This spirit, dumb to us, will speak to him.
Do you consent we shall acquaint him with it,
As needful in our loves, fitting our duty?

   Marcellus. Let's do't, I pray; and I this morning know
Where we shall find him most conveniently.   [*Exeunt.*

Scene II.   *A Room of State in the Castle.*

Enter the KING, QUEEN, HAMLET, POLONIUS, LAERTES, VOLTIMAND,
CORNELIUS, Lords, *and* Attendants.

   King. Though yet of Hamlet our dear brother's death
The memory be green, and that it us befitted
To bear our hearts in grief, and our whole kingdom
To be contracted in one brow of woe;
Yet so far hath discretion fought with nature,

   [1] " Made probation," i.e., gave proof.
   [2] " Planets strike," alluding to the old astrological belief of the malign
influence of the planets.
   [3] Blasts, or infects with disease.

That we with wisest sorrow think on him,
Together with remembrance of ourselves.
Therefore our sometime sister, now our Queen,
Th' imperial jointress [1] to this warlike State,
Have we, as 'twere with a defeated joy,—
With one auspicious [2] and one dropping [3] eye,
With mirth in funeral, and with dirge in marriage,
In equal scale weighing delight and dole, [4]—
Taken to wife: nor have we herein barr'd
Your better wisdoms, which have freely gone
With this affair along.   For all, our thanks.
Now follows, that you know, young Fortinbras,
Holding a weak supposal of our worth,
Or thinking by our late dear brother's death
Our State to be disjoint and out of frame,
Colleagued [5] with the dream of his advantage,
He hath not fail'd to pester us with message,
Importing the surrender of those lands
Lost by his father, with all bonds of law,
To our most valiant brother.   So much for him.
Now for ourself and for this time of meeting.
Thus much the business is: we have here writ
To Norway, uncle of young Fortinbras,—
Who, impotent and bedrid, scarcely hears
Of this his nephew's purpose,— to suppress
His further gait [6] herein; in that the levies,
The lists and full proportions, are all made
Out of his subject: and we here dispatch
You, good Cornelius, and you, Voltimand,

1 Joint possessor.   2 Cheerful.
3 Shedding sorrowful tears.
4 Grief.
5 Having for his only ally in the enterprise the advantage he fondly imagines he will derive from this state of affairs.
6 Proceeding.

For bearers of this greeting to old Norway;
Giving to you no further personal power
To business with the King, more than the scope
Of these dilated articles allow.[1]
Farewell, and let your haste commend your duty.

   Cornelius.   }
   Voltimand. } In that and all things will we show our duty.

   King. We doubt it nothing. Heartily farewell.

                      [Exeunt Voltimand and Cornelius.

And now, Laertes, what's the news with you?
You told us of some suit; what is't, Laertes?
You cannot speak of reason to the Dane,
And lose your voice: what wouldst thou beg, Laertes,
That shall not be my offer, not thy asking?
The head is not more native to the heart,
The hand more instrumental to the mouth,
Than is the throne of Denmark to thy father.
What wouldst thou have, Laertes?

   Laertes.   My dread lord,
Your leave and favor to return to France;
From whence though willingly I came to Denmark,
To show my duty in your coronation,
Yet now, I must confess, that duty done,
My thoughts and wishes bend again toward France,
And bow them to your gracious leave and pardon.[2]

   King. Have you your father's leave?—What says Polonius?

   Polonius. He hath, my lord, wrung from me my slow leave
By laborsome petition, and at last
Upon his will I seal'd my hard[3] consent:
I do beseech you, give him leave to go.

   King. Take thy fair hour, Laertes; time be thine,

---

[1] " More than the scope," etc., i.e., more than is comprised in the general
design of these articles, which you may set forth more in detail.

[2] " And bow," etc., i.e., and humbly beg your permission to depart.

[3] Reluctant.

And thy best graces spend it at thy will ! [1] —
But now, my cousin [2] Hamlet, and my son, —

Hamlet. [*Aside*] <u>A little more than kin, and less than kind.</u>[3]

King. How is it that the clouds still hang on you ?

Hamlet. Not so, my lord; I am too much i' the sun.[4]

Queen. Good Hamlet, cast thy nighted color off,
And let thine eye look like a friend on Denmark.
Do not forever with thy vailed lids [5]
Seek for thy noble father in the dust :
Thou know'st 'tis common; all that lives must die,
Passing through nature to eternity.

Hamlet. Ay, madam, it is common.

Queen.   If it be,
Why seems it so particular with thee ?

Hamlet. Seems, madam ! nay, it is; I know not " seems."
'Tis not alone my inky cloak, good mother,
Nor customary suits of solemn black,
Nor windy suspiration of forc'd breath,[6]
No, nor the fruitful river in the eye,
Nor the dejected 'havior of the visage,
Together with all forms, modes, shapes of grief,
That can denote me truly : these indeed seem,
For they are actions that a man might play :
But I have that within which passeth show;
These but the trappings and the suits of woe.

King. 'Tis sweet and com'mendable in your nature, Hamlet,
To give these mourning duties to your father :

---

[1] " Time be thine," etc., i.e., may the exercise of thy virtues fill up thy time, which is wholly at thy will.

[2] Used by Shakespeare for any degree of relationship beyond the first.

[3] Malone has this paraphrase : " I am a little more than thy kinsman, for I am thy stepson ; and am somewhat less than kind to thee, for I hate thee as being the person who has incestuously married my mother."

[4] The allusion is probably to the old proverb : " Out of God's blessing into the warm sun."

[5] " Vailed lids," i.e., drooping eyes.   [6] Insincere sighs.

But, you must know, your father lost a father;
That father lost, lost his; and the survivor bound
In filial obligation for some term
To do obsequious sorrow :[1] but to persev'er
In obstinate condolement [2] is a course
Of impious stubbornness; 'tis unmanly grief;
It shows a will most incorrect to Heaven,
A heart unfortified, a mind impatient,
An understanding simple [3] and unschool'd:
For what we know must be, and is as common
As any the most vulgar thing to sense,
Why should we in our peevish [4] opposition
Take it to heart ?   Fie ! 'tis a fault to Heaven,
A fault against the dead, a fault to nature,
To reason most absurd; whose common theme
Is death of fathers, and who still hath cried,
From the first corse till he that died to-day,
"This must be so."   We pray you, throw to earth
This unprevailing [5] woe, and think of us
As of a father; for let the world take note,
You are the most immediate to our throne;
And with no less nobility of love
Than that which dearest father bears his son,
Do I impart toward you.   For your intent
In going back to school in Wittenberg,
It is most retrograde [6] to our desire;
And we beseech you, bend you to remain
Here, in the cheer and comfort of our eye,
Our chiefest courtier, cousin, and our son.

 Queen.   Let not thy mother lose her prayers, Hamlet:
I pray thee, stay with us; go not to Wittenberg.

---

[1] " Obsequious sorrow," i.e., the sorrow that pertains to the obsequies, or funeral ceremonies.

[2] Grief.   [3] Weak.   [4] Fretful.
[5] Unavailing.   [6] Opposed.

Hamlet. I shall in all my best obey you, madam.

King. Why, 'tis a loving and a fair reply:
Be as ourself in Denmark. — Madam, come;
This gentle and unforc'd accord of Hamlet
Sits smiling to my heart; in græce whereof,
No jocund health that Denmark [1] drinks to-day,
But the great cannon to the clouds shall tell,
And the King's rouse [2] the heavens shall bruit again, [3]
Respeaking earthly thunder. Come away.

[Exeunt all but Hamlet.

Hamlet. O that this too, too solid flesh would melt,
Thaw, and resolve [4] itself into a dew !
Or that the Everlasting had not fix'd
His canon 'gainst self-slaughter ! O God ! God !
How weary, stale, flat, and unprofitable,
Seem to me all the uses of this world !
Fie on't ! ah, fie ! 'tis an unweeded garden,
That grows to seed; things rank and gross in nature
Possess it merely. [5] That it should come to this !
But two months dead ! nay, not so much, not two:
So excellent a king; that was, to this,
Hyperion [6] to a satyr; [7] so loving to my mother
That he might not beteem [8] the winds of heaven
Visit her face too roughly. Heaven and earth !
Must I remember ? why, she would hang on him,
As if increase of appetite had grown

[1] The King of Denmark.

[2] Carousal, or drinking bout.   [3] " Bruit again," i.e., echo.

[4] Dissolve.   [5] Completely.

[6] Hyperion, by which name Apollo was sometimes called, was, according to classic mythology, the god of day, and the most perfect in form and feature of all the gods.

[7] The satyrs were fabulous creatures, "represented like men, but with the feet and legs of goats, short horns on the head, and the whole body covered with thick hair."

[8] Allow.

By what it fed on; and yet, within a month, —
Let me not think on't — Frailty, thy name is woman!
A little month, or ere those shoes were old
With which she follow'd my poor father's body,
Like Niobe,[1] all tears, — why she, even she, —
O God! a beast, that wants discourse of reason,[2]
Would have mourn'd longer, — married with my uncle,
My father's brother, but no more like my father
Than I to Hercules:[3] within a month;
Ere yet the salt of most unrighteous tears
Had left the flushing in her galled eyes,
She married.   O, most wicked speed, to post
With such dexterity to a second match!
It is not, nor it cannot come to, good:
But break, my heart; for I must hold my tongue.

Enter HORATIO, MARCELLUS, *and* BERNARDO.

Horatio. Hail to your lordship!
Hamlet.   I am glad to see you well.
Horatio, — or I do forget myself.
Horatio. The same, my lord, and your poor servant ever.
Hamlet. Sir, my good friend; I'll change that name with you.
And what make you[4] from Wittenberg, Horatio? —
Marcellus?

---

[1] Niobe having grievously insulted Apollo and Diana, they avenged the affront on her fourteen children. Her sons were slain by Apollo while they were hunting in the forest. Diana pursued the daughters, who one by one fell, never to rise again. The youngest clung to her mother's breast; but even there death found and claimed her. "Then the gods, touched by the sight of woe so intense, changed Niobe into stone. . . . This statue was placed on Mount Sipylus, . . . and it was said that tears continually flowed down the marble cheeks; for, though changed, Niobe still felt, and wept for her great loss."— GUERBER: *Myths of Greece and Rome*, p. 94.

[2] "Discourse of reason," i.e., the reasoning faculty.

[3] A fabulous hero of antiquity, renowned for his courage and strength.

[4] "What make you?" i.e., what are you doing?

Marcellus. My good lord—

Hamlet. I am very glad to see you. — Good even, sir.[1]
But what, in faith, make you from Wittenberg?

Horatio. A truant disposition, good my lord.

Hamlet. I would not hear your enemy say so,
Nor shall you do mine ear that violence,
To make it truster of your own report
Against yourself: I know you are no truant.
But what is your affair in Elsinore?
We'll teach you to drink deep ere you depart.

Horatio. My lord, I came to see your father's funeral.

Hamlet. I pray thee, do not mock me, fellow-student;
I think it was to see my mother's wedding.

Horatio. Indeed, my lord, it follow'd hard upon.

Hamlet. Thrift, thrift, Horatio!   The funeral bak'd meats[2]
Did coldly furnish forth the marriage tables.
Would I had met my dearest[3] foe in heaven
Or ever I had seen that day, Horatio!
My father!—methinks I see my father.

Horatio. Where, my lord?

Hamlet.   In my mind's eye, Horatio.

Horatio. I saw him once; he was a goodly king.

Hamlet. He was a man, take him for all in all,
I shall not look upon his like again.

Horatio. My lord, I think I saw him yesternight.

Hamlet. Saw who?[4]

Horatio. My lord, the King your father.

Hamlet.   The King my father!

Horatio. Season your admiration for a while

---

1 Addressed to Bernardo.

2 It was anciently the general custom to give a cold entertainment to mourners at a funeral.

3 " Shakespeare uses ' dear ' for whatever touches us nearly, either in love or hate, joy or sorrow." — CLARK and WRIGHT.

4 Whom.

With an attent ear,[1] till I may deliver,
Upon the witness of these gentlemen,
This marvel to you.

 Hamlet.   For God's love, let me hear.

 Horatio. Two nights together had these gentlemen,
Marcellus and Bernardo, on their watch,
In the dead vast[2] and middle of the night,
Been thus encounter'd. A figure like your father,
Armed at point[3] exactly, cap-a-pie,[4]
Appears before them, and with solemn march
Goes slow and stately by them: thrice he walk'd
By their oppress'd and fear-surprised eyes,
Within his truncheon's[5] length; whilst they, distill'd
Almost to jelly with the act[6] of fear,
Stand dumb, and speak not to him. This to me
In dreadful secrecy impart they did;
And I with them the third night kept the watch:
Where, as they had deliver'd, both in time,
Form of the thing, each word made true and good,
The apparition comes. I knew your father;
These hands are not more like.

 Hamlet.   But where was this?

 Marcellus. My lord, upon the platform where we watch'd.

 Hamlet. Did you not speak to it?

 Horatio.   My lord, I did;
But answer made it none: yet once methought
It lifted up its head, and did address
Itself to motion, like as it would speak;
But even then the morning cock crew loud,

---

[1] "Season your admiration," etc., i.e., let your wonder be qualified by your attention for a time.

[2] Emptiness; vacancy.

[3] At all points.   [4] From head to foot.

[5] A short staff, a symbol of office.

[6] Action.

And at the sound it shrunk in haste away,
And vanish'd from our sight.

 Hamlet.   'Tis very strange.

 Horatio. As I do live, my honor'd lord, 'tis true;
And we did think it writ down in our duty
To let you know of it.

 Hamlet. Indeed, indeed, sirs, but this troubles me.
Hold you the watch to-night?

 Marcellus. }
 Bernardo. }   We do, my lord.

 Hamlet. Arm'd, say you?

 Marcellus. }
 Bernardo. }   Arm'd, my lord.

 Hamlet.   From top to toe?

 Marcellus. }
 Bernardo. } My lord, from head to foot.

 Hamlet.   Then saw you not his face?

 Horatio. O, yes, my lord; he wore his beaver [1] up.

 Hamlet. What, look'd he frowningly?

 Horatio. A countenance more in sorrow than in anger.

 Hamlet. Pale, or red?

 Horatio. Nay, very pale.

 Hamlet.   And fix'd his eyes upon you?

 Horatio. Most constantly.

 Hamlet.   I would I had been there.

 Horatio. It would have much amaz'd you.

 Hamlet. Very like, very like. Stay'd it long?

 Horatio. While one with moderate haste might tell [2] a hundred.

 Marcellus. }
 Bernardo. } Longer, longer.

 Horatio. Not when I saw't.

 Hamlet.   His beard was grizzl'd? no?

---

[1] A movable front of the helmet, which could be drawn above the face, or used to protect it.

[2] Count.

Horatio. It was, as I have seen it in his life,
A sable silver'd.

Hamlet.   I will watch to-night;
Perchance 'twill walk again.

Horatio.   I warrant it will.

Hamlet. If it assume my noble father's person,
I'll speak to it, though hell itself should gape
And bid me hold my peace.   I pray you all,
If you have hitherto conceal'd this sight,
Let it be tenable [1] in your silence still;
And whatsoever else shall hap to-night,
Give it an understanding, but no tongue:
I will requite your loves.   So, fare you well:
Upon the platform, 'twixt eleven and twelve,
I'll visit you.

All.   Our duty to your honor.

Hamlet. Your loves, as mine to you.   Farewell.

                      [*Exeunt all but Hamlet.*

My father's spirit in arms! all is not well;
I doubt some foul play: would the night were come!
Till then sit still, my soul: foul deeds will rise,
Though all the earth o'erwhelm them, to men's eyes.   [*Exit.*

SCENE III. *A Room in Polonius' House.*

Enter LAERTES *and* OPHELIA.

Laertes. My necessaries are embark'd:[2] farewell:
And, sister, as the winds give benefit
And convoy [3] is assistant, do not sleep,
But let me hear from you.

Ophelia.   Do you doubt that?

[1] Held.

[2] " My necessaries are embark'd," i.e., my baggage is on board the vessel.

[3] Means of conveyance.

Laertes. For Hamlet and the trifling of his favor,
Hold it a fashion, and a toy in blood,[1]
A violet in the youth of primy nature,
Forward, not permanent, sweet, not lasting,
The perfume and suppliance of a minute;
No more.

   Ophelia. No more but so?

   Laertes.   Think it no more:
For nature, crescent,[2] does not grow alone
In thews and bulk; but, as this temple waxes,[3]
The inward service of the mind and soul
Grows wide withal.   Perhaps he loves you now,
And now no soil nor cautel[4] doth besmirch
The virtue of his will: but you must fear,
His greatness weigh'd, his will is not his own;
For he himself is subject to his birth.
He may not, as unvalued persons do,
Carve for himself; for on his choice depends
The safety and the health of the whole State;
And therefore must his choice be circumscrib'd
Unto the voice and yielding of that body
Whereof he is the head.[5]   Then if he says he loves you,
It fits your wisdom so far to believe it
As he in his particular act and place
May give his saying deed; which is no further
Than the main voice of Denmark goes withal.
Then weigh what loss your honor may sustain,
If with too credent[6] ear you list his songs.

---

  1 " A fashion," etc., i.e., merely a temporary pastime and impulse.

  2 Increasing.

  3 " Temple waxes," i.e., body grows.

  4 Crafty design.

  5 " His choice be circumscrib'd," etc., i.e., he may not choose (a wife)
without the approving voice of the nation of which he is the head.

  6 Credulous.

Fear it, Ophelia, fear it, my dear sister,
And keep you in the rear of your affection,
Out of the shot and danger of desire.
The chariest maid is prodigal enough,
If she unmask her beauty to the moon.
Virtue itself 'scapes not calumnious strokes:
The canker [1] galls the infants of the spring,
Too oft before their buttons be disclos'd; [2]
And in the morn and liquid dew of youth
Contagious blastments [3] are most imminent.
Be wary, then; best safety lies in fear.
Youth to itself rebels, though none else near.

 Ophelia. I shall the effect of this good lesson keep,
As watchman to my heart.   But, good my brother,
Do not, as some ungracious pastors do,
Show me the steep and thorny way to heaven,
Whiles, like a puff'd and reckless libertine,
Himself the primrose path of dalliance treads,
And recks not his own rede. [4]

 Laertes.   O, fear me not.
I stay too long: but here my father comes.

     Enter POLONIUS.

A double blessing is a double grace;
Occasion smiles upon a second leave.

 Polonius. Yet here, Laertes? aboard, aboard, for shame!
The wind sits in the shoulder of your sail,
And you are stay'd for.   There; my blessing with thee!
And these few precepts in thy memory
See thou charac'ter. [5]   Give thy thoughts no tongue,

 [1] Cankerworm.

 [2] " Buttons be disclos'd," i.e., buds are opened.

 [3] " Contagious blastments," i.e., pernicious blights.

 [4] " Recks not his own rede," i.e., regards not his own advice.

 [5] Engrave.

Nor any unproportion'd thought his [1] act.
Be thou familiar, but by no means vulgar.
Those friends thou hast, and their adoption tried,
Grapple them to thy soul with hoops of steel;
But do not dull thy palm with entertainment
Of each new-hatch'd, unfledg'd comrade'.   Beware
Of entrance to a quarrel, but being in,
Bear't that the opposed may beware of thee.
Give every man thy ear, but few thy voice;
Take each man's censure,[2] but reserve thy judgment.
Costly thy habit as thy purse can buy,
But not express'd in fancy; rich, not gaudy;
For the apparel oft proclaims the man,
And they in France of the best rank and station
Are most select and generous, chief in that.
Neither a borrower nor a lender be;
For loan oft loses both itself and friend,
And borrowing dulls the edge of husbandry.[3]
This above all: to thine own self be true,
And it must follow, as the night the day,
Thou canst not then be false to any man.
Farewell: my blessing season [4] this in thee !

    Laertes. Most humbly do I take my leave, my lord.
    Polonius. The time invites you: go; your servants tend.
    Laertes. Farewell, Ophelia; and remember well
What I have said to you.
    Ophelia.   'Tis in my memory lock'd,
And you yourself shall keep the key of it.
    Laertes. Farewell.   [*Exit.*
    Polonius. What is't, Ophelia, he hath said to you ?

---

  1 " His " was formerly neuter as well as masculine, or the possessive of
" it " as well as of " he," and is so used by the Elizabethan writers generally;
though " its " is met with occasionally in Shakespeare.
  2 Opinion.   3 Economy.
  4 Make durable.

Ophelia. So please you, something touching the Lord Hamlet.

Polonius. Marry,[1] well bethought:

'Tis told me, he hath very oft of late

Given private time to you; and you yourself

Have of your audience been most free and bounteous.

If it be so, as so 'tis put on me,

And that in way of caution, I must tell you,

You do not understand yourself so clearly

As it behooves my daughter and your honor.

What is between you? give me up the truth.

Ophelia. He hath, my lord, of late made many tenders

Of his affection to me.

Polonius. Affection! pooh! you speak like a green girl,

Unsifted in such perilous circumstance.

Do you believe his tenders, as you call them?

Ophelia. I do not know, my lord, what I should think.

Polonius. Marry, I'll teach you: think yourself a baby;

That you have ta'en these tenders for true pay,

Which are not sterling.[2] Tender yourself more dearly;

Or—not to crack the wind of the poor phrase,

Running it thus—you'll tender me a fool.

Ophelia. My lord, he hath impor'tun'd me with love

In honorable fashion.

Polonius. Ay, fashion you may call it; go to, go to![3]

Ophelia. And hath given countenance to his speech, my lord,

With almost all the holy vows of Heaven.

Polonius. Ay, springes to catch woodcocks.[4] I do know,

When the blood burns, how prodigal the soul

---

[1] This petty oath is a corruption of the name of the Virgin Mary.

[2] "Not sterling," i.e., not true value.

[3] "Go to" is an exclamation with many phases of meaning as used by old writers, — of reproach, of encouragement, of contempt, of impatience, etc.

[4] "Springes to catch woodcocks:" the woodcock is a silly bird, and the popular belief was, that it had no brains. Hence this proverb applied to a person easily deceived.

Lends the tongue vows: these blazes, daughter,
Giving more light than heat, extinct in both,
Even in their promise, as it is a-making,
You must not take for fire.   From this time
Be somewhat scanter of your maiden presence;
Set your entreatments [1] at a higher rate
Than a command to parley.   For Lord Hamlet,
Believe so much in him, that he is young,
And with a larger tether may he walk
Than may be given you: in few, Ophelia,
Do not believe his vows; for they are brokers,[2]
Not of that dye which their investments [3] show,
But mere implorators [4] of unholy suits,
Breathing like sanctified and pious bawds,
The better to beguile.   This is for all:
I would not, in plain terms, from this time forth,
Have you so slander [5] any moment's leisure
As to give words or talk with the Lord Hamlet.
Look to't, I charge you: come your ways.
    Ophelia. I shall obey, my lord.   [*Exeunt.*

SCENE IV.   *The Platform.*

Enter HAMLET, HORATIO, *and* MARCELLUS.

Hamlet. The air bites shrewdly; it is very cold.
Horatio. It is a nipping and an eager air.
Hamlet. What hour now?
Horatio.   I think it lacks of twelve.
Marcellus. No, it is struck.
Horatio. Indeed? I heard it not: it then draws near the season
Wherein the spirit held his wont to walk.
          [*A flourish of trumpets, and ordnance shot off, within.*
What does this mean, my lord?

1 Invitations you receive.   2 Negotiators.
3 Dress, or outward appearance.   4 Solicitors.   5 Misuse.

Hamlet. The King doth wake to-night, and takes his rouse,
Keeps wassail,[1] and the swaggering upspring[2] reels;
And, as he drains his draughts of Rhenish[3] down,
The kettledrum and trumpet thus bray out
The triumph of his pledge.

Horatio.   Is it a custom?

Hamlet. Ay, marry, is't;
But to my mind, though I am native here
And to the manner born, it is a custom
More honor'd in the breach than the observance.
This heavy-headed revel east and west
Makes us traduc'd and tax'd[4] of other nations:
They clepe[5] us drunkards, and with swinish phrase
Soil our addition;[6] and indeed it takes
From our achievements, though perform'd at height,
The pith and marrow of our attribute.[7]
So, oft it chances in particular men,
That for some vicious mole of nature[8] in them,
As, in their birth, — wherein they are not guilty,
Since nature cannot choose his origin, —
By the o'ergrowth of some complexion,[9]
Oft breaking down the pales and forts of reason,
Or by some habit that too much o'erleavens
The form of plausive[10] manners, that these men,
Carrying, I say, the stamp of one defect,
Being nature's livery, or fortune's star,[11] —
Their virtues else, be they as pure as grace,
As infinite as man may undergo,

[1] Revelry.

[2] "Upspring" was a wild and boisterous German dance.

[3] Rhine wine.   [4] Censured.   [5] Call.

[6] Title.   [7] Reputation.

[8] "Vicious mole of nature," i.e., some natural taint.

[9] Temperament or humor; as melancholy, sanguine, etc.

[10] Pleasing.

[11] "Nature's livery," etc., i.e., a natural or accidental blemish.

Shall in the general censure [1] take corruption
From that particular fault: the dram of base
Doth all the noble substance often dout [2]
To his own scandal.

    Horatio.   Look, my lord, it comes !

                 Enter GHOST.

    Hamlet.   Angels and ministers of grace defend us !
Be thou a spirit of health, or goblin damn'd,
Bring with thee airs from heaven, or blasts from hell,
Be thy intents wicked, or charitable,
Thou com'st in such a questionable [3] shape
That I will speak to thee: I'll call thee Hamlet,
King, father, royal Dane: O, answer me !
Let me not burst in ignorance; but tell
Why thy canon'iz'd bones, hearsed in death,
Have burst their cerements; [4] why the sepulcher,
Wherein we saw thee quietly inurn'd,
Hath op'd his ponderous and marble jaws
To cast thee up again.   What may this mean,
That thou, dead corse, again in com'plete steel
Revisit'st thus the glimpses of the moon,
Making night hideous; and we fools of nature
So horridly to shake our disposition
With thoughts beyond the reaches of our souls ?
Say, why is this ? wherefore ? what should we do ?

                     [*Ghost beckons Hamlet.*

    Horatio.   It beckons you to go away with it,
As if it some impartment did desire
To you alone.

---

   [1] Judgment.   [2] Do out; smother; extinguish.
   [3] Inviting question.
   [4] Waxed cloths wrapped around the corpse, or with which the coffin was
lined.

Marcellus.   Look, with what courteous action
It waves you to a more removed[1] ground:
But do not go with it.
   Horatio.   No, by no means.
   Hamlet. It will not speak; then I will follow it.
   Horatio. Do not, my lord.
   Hamlet.   Why, what should be the fear?
I do not set my life at a pin's fee;[2]
And for my soul, what can it do to that,
Being a thing immortal as itself?
It waves me forth again: I'll follow it.
   Horatio. What if it tempt you toward the flood, my lord,
Or to the dreadful summit of the cliff
That beetles o'er[3] his base into the sea,
And there assume some other horrible form,
Which might deprive your sovereignty of reason,[4]
And draw you into madness? think of it:
The very place puts toys of desperation,[5]
Without more motive, into every brain
That looks so many fathoms to the sea,
And hears it roar beneath.
   Hamlet.   It waves me still.—
Go on: I'll follow thee.
   Marcellus. You shall not go, my lord.
   Hamlet.   Hold off your hands.
   Horatio. Be rul'd; you shall not go.
   Hamlet.   My fate cries out,
And makes each petty artery in this body
As hardy as the Nemean lion's[6] nerve.

---

[1] Remote.   [2] "Pin's fee," i.e., pin's value.
[3] "Beetles o'er," i.e., leans over.
[4] "Deprive your sovereignty of reason," i.e., take from you the controlling power of your reason.
[5] "Toys of desperation," i.e., desperate fancies.
[6] "Nemean lion," i.e., the fierce beast of Nemea, which, we are told,

Still am I call'd. Unhand me, gentlemen.
By Heaven, I'll make a ghost of him that lets [1] me !
I say, away !—Go on: I'll follow thee.

                            [Exeunt Ghost and Hamlet.

   Horatio. He waxes desperate with imagination.
   Marcellus. Let's follow; 'tis not fit thus to obey him.
   Horatio. Have after.[2] To what issue will this come ?
   Marcellus. Something is rotten in the state of Denmark.
   Horatio. Heaven will direct it.
   Marcellus.   Nay, let's follow him. *[Exeunt.*

SCENE V. *Another Part of the Platform.*

Enter GHOST *and* HAMLET.

   Hamlet. Where wilt thou lead me? speak : I'll go no farther.
   Ghost. Mark me.
   Hamlet.   I will.
   Ghost.   My hour is almost come,
When I to sulphurous and tormenting flames
Must render up myself.
   Hamlet.   Alas, poor ghost !
   Ghost. Pity me not, but lend thy serious hearing
To what I shall unfold.
   Hamlet.   Speak ; I am bound to hear.
   Ghost. So art thou to revenge, when thou shalt hear.
   Hamlet. What ?
   Ghost. I am thy father's spirit,
Doom'd for a certain term to walk the night,
And for the day confin'd to fast in fires,

Hercules (see Note 3, p. 32) attacked with a club, and finally choked to
death.

  [1] Hinders.
  [2] " Have after," i.e., we'll follow him.

Till the foul crimes done in my days of nature
Are burnt and purg'd away.   But that I am forbid
To tell the secrets of my prison house,
I could a tale unfold whose lightest word
Would harrow up [1] thy soul, freeze thy young blood,
Make thy two eyes, like stars, start from their spheres,
Thy knotted and combined locks to part,
And each particular hair to stand an end,
Like quills upon the fretful porpentine: [2]
But this eternal [3] blazon [4] must not be
To ears of flesh and blood.   List, list, O, list !
If thou didst ever thy dear father love—
    Hamlet. O God !
    Ghost. Revenge his foul and most unnatural murder.
    Hamlet. Murder !
    Ghost. Murder most foul, as in the best it is ;
But this most foul, strange, and unnatural.
    Hamlet. Haste me to know't, that I, with wings as swift
As meditation or the thoughts of love,
May sweep to my revenge.
    Ghost.   I find thee apt ;
And duller shouldst thou be than the fat weed
That roots itself in ease on Lethe [5] wharf,
Wouldst thou not stir in this.   Now, Hamlet, hear:
'Tis given out that, sleeping in my orchard,
A serpent stung me ; so the whole ear of Denmark
Is by a forged process [6] of my death

   [1] " Harrow up," i.e., lacerate.

   [2] Porcupine.

   [3] " Eternal " has the sense of " infernal " here, as in other passages of
Shakespeare.

   [4] Revelation.

   [5] The river of oblivion.   A mythological river of the Lower World, the
waters of which had the effect of making those who drank them forget all they
had seen, heard, or done before.

   [6] " Forged process," i.e., false report of the cause.

Rankly abus'd : but know, thou noble youth,
The serpent that did sting thy father's life
Now wears his crown.

    Hamlet.   O my prophetic soul !
My uncle !

    Ghost. Ay, that incestuous, that adulterate beast,
With witchcraft of his wit, with traitorous gifts,—
O wicked wit and gifts, that have the power
So to seduce !—won to his shameful lust
The will of my most seeming-virtuous queen.
O Hamlet, what a falling off was there !
From me, whose love was of that dignity
That it went hand in hand even with the vow
I made to her in marriage, and to decline
Upon a wretch whose natural gifts were poor
To those of mine!
But, soft ! methinks I scent the morning air ;
Brief let me be.   Sleeping within my orchard,
My custom always of the afternoon,
Upon my se'cure hour thy uncle stole,
With juice of cursed hebenon [1] in a vial,
And in the porches of my ears [2] did pour
The leperous distilment ; whose effect
Holds such an enmity with blood of man
That swift as quicksilver it courses through
The natural gates and alleys of the body,
And with a sudden vigor it doth posset
And curd, like eager droppings into milk,
The thin and wholesome blood.   So did it mine ;

---

  1 Henbane.
  2 "And in the porches of my ears," etc., Furness (Variorum Shakespeare,
vol. iii. p. 102) quotes Caldecott's note : " The medical professors of Shakespeare's day believed that poison might be introduced into the system through
the ears.   The eminent surgeon Ambroise Paré . . . was suspected of having,
when he dressed the ear of Francis II., poured poison into it."

And a most instant tetter bark'd about,[1]
Most lazar-like, with vile and loathsome crust,
All my smooth body.
Thus was I, sleeping, by a brother's hand,
Of life, of crown, of queen, at once dispatch'd:
Cut off even in the blossoms of my sin,
Unhousel'd,[2] disappointed,[3] unanel'd;[4]
No reck'ning made, but sent to my account
With all my imperfections on my head:
O, horrible!   O, horrible! most horrible!
If thou hast nature in thee, bear it not.
But, howsoever thou pursu'st this act,
Taint not thy mind, nor let thy soul contrive
Against thy mother aught: leave her to Heaven,
And to those thorns that in her bosom lodge,
To prick and sting her.   Fare thee well at once!
The glowworm shows the matin[5] to be near,
And 'gins to pale his uneffectual[6] fire.
Adieu, adieu!   Hamlet, remember me.   [*Exit.*

   Hamlet. O all you host of heaven!   O earth! what else?
And shall I couple hell?   O, fie!   Hold, hold, my heart;
And you, my sinews, grow not instant old,
But bear me stiffly up. — Remember thee!
Ay, thou poor ghost, while memory holds a seat
In this distracted globe.[7]   Remember thee!
Yea, from the table of my memory
I'll wipe away all trivial fond[8] records',
All saws[9] of books, all forms, all pressures[10] past,

---

1 " Bark'd about," i.e., covered as with a bark.
2 Without having received the sacrament administered to the dying.
3 Unprepared.   4 Without having received extreme unction.
5 Morning.   6 Ineffectual.
7 " In this distracted globe," i.e., in this frenzied brain (pointing to his head).   8 Foolish.
9 Proverbs.   10 Impressions.

That youth and observation copied there;
And thy commandment all alone shall live
Within the book and volume of my brain,
Unmix'd with baser matter: yes, by Heaven!
O most pernicious woman!
O villain, villain, smiling, damned villain!
My tables,[1]—meet it is I set it down,
That one may smile, and smile, and be a villain:
At least I'm sure it may be so in Denmark. —   [*Writing.*
So, uncle, there you are. — Now to my word;
It is "Adieu, adieu!   Remember me."
I have sworn't.

Marcellus. ⎫
Horatio.   ⎬ [*Within*] My lord, my lord —

Marcellus.   [*Within*] Lord Hamlet—
Horatio.   [*Within*] Heaven secure him!
Hamlet. So be it!
Horatio. [*Within*] Hillo, ho, ho, my lord!
Hamlet. Hillo, ho, ho, boy! come, bird, come.[2]

Enter HORATIO *and* MARCELLUS.

Marcellus. How is't, my noble lord?
Horatio.   What news, my lord?
Hamlet. O, wonderful!
Horatio.   Good my lord, tell it.
Hamlet. No; you'll reveal it.
Horatio. Not I, my lord, by Heaven.
Marcellus.   Nor I, my lord.
Hamlet. How say you, then; would heart of man once think it?
But you'll be secret?

Horatio.   ⎫
Marcellus. ⎬   Ay, by Heaven, my lord.

1 Tablets.
2 " Hillo, ho," etc., i.e., the cry which the falconer uses to his hawk when
he would have it come down to him.

Hamlet. There's ne'er a villain dwelling in all Denmark
But he's an arrant knave.

Horatio. There needs no ghost, my lord, come from the grave
To tell us this.

Hamlet.   Why, right; you are i' the right;
And so, without more circumstance [1] at all,
I hold it fit that we shake hands, and part:
You, as your business and desire shall point you; —
For every man has business and desire,
Such as it is; — and for mine own poor part,
Look you, I'll go pray.

Horatio. These are but wild and whirling [2] words, my lord.

Hamlet. I'm sorry they offend you, heartily;
Yes, 'faith, heartily.

Horatio.   There's no offense, my lord.

Hamlet. Yes, by Saint Patrick, but there is, Horatio,
And much offense too.   Touching this vision here,
It is an honest ghost, that let me tell you:
For your desire to know what is between us,
O'ermaster't as you may.   And now, good friends,
As you are friends, scholars, and soldiers,
Give me one poor request.

Horatio. What is't, my lord? we will.

Hamlet. Never make known what you have seen to-night.

Horatio.
Marcellus. } My lord, we will not.

Hamlet.   Nay, but swear't.

Horatio.   In faith,
My lord, not I.

Marcellus.   Nor I, my lord, in faith.

Hamlet. Upon my sword. [3]

1 " More circumstance," i.e., more ado.

2 Extravagant.

3 The sword's hilt was in the form of a cross: hence the custom of swear
ing on the sword.

Marcellus.   We have sworn, my lord, already.

Hamlet. Indeed, upon my sword, indeed.

Ghost. [*Beneath*] Swear.

Hamlet. Ah, ha, boy! say'st thou so? art thou there, true-
    penny?—

Come on—you hear this fellow in the cellarage,—

Consent to swear.

Horatio.   Propose the oath, my lord.

Hamlet. Never to speak of this that you have seen.

Swear by my sword.

Ghost. [*Beneath*] Swear.

Hamlet. Hic et ubique? [1] then we'll shift our ground.

Come hither, gentlemen,

And lay your hands again upon my sword,

Never to speak of this that you have heard,

Swear by my sword.

Ghost. [*Beneath*] Swear.

Hamlet. Well said, old mole! canst work i' the earth so fast?

A worthy pioner! [2]—Once more remove, good friends.

Horatio. O day and night, but this is wondrous strange!

Hamlet. And therefore as a stranger give it welcome.

There are more things in heaven and earth, Horatio,

Than are dreamt of in your philosophy. [3]

But come;

Here, as before, never, so help you mercy,

How strange or odd soe'er I bear myself,

As I perchance hereafter shall think meet

To put an antic disposition [4] on,

---

[1] "Hic et ubique" (Latin), i.e., here and everywhere.

[2] Pioneer. It is the duty of the pioneers of an army to go in advance of the main body of troops, and by felling trees, etc., clear the way of obstacles that would impede the march.

[3] "Your philosophy:" "your" is used colloquially here, and "philosophy" is the emphatic word.

[4] "Antic disposition," i.e., fantastic behavior.

That you, at such times seeing me, never shall,
With arms encumber'd thus, or this headshake,
Or by pronouncing of some doubtful phrase,
As, "Well, well, we know," or "We could, an if [1] we would,"
Or "If we list to speak," or "There be, an if they might,"
Or such ambiguous giving out, to note
That you know aught of me : this not to do,
So grace and mercy at your most need help you,
Swear.

    Ghost. [*Beneath*] Swear.

    Hamlet. Rest, rest, perturbed spirit ! [*They swear.*] So, gen-
        tlemen,
With all my love I do commend me to you;
And what so poor a man as Hamlet is
May do to express his love and friending to you,
God willing, shall not lack.   Let us go in together;
And still your fingers on your lips, I pray.
The time is out of joint : O cursed spite,
That ever I was born to set it right !
Nay, come, let's go together.   [*Exeunt*

ACT II.

Scene I.   *A Room in Polonius' House.*

Enter Polonius *and* Reynaldo.

Polonius. Give him this money and these notes, Reynaldo.

Reynaldo. I will, my lord.

Polonius. You shall do marvelous wisely, good Reynaldo,
Before you visit him, to make inquire [2]
Of his behavior.

Reynaldo.   My lord, I did intend it.

    [1] " An if," i.e., if.   [2] Inquiry.

Polonius. Marry, well said; very well said. Look you, sir,
Inquire me first what Danskers[1] are in Paris;
And how, and who, what means, and where they keep,[2]
What company, at what expense; and finding
By this encompassment[3] and drift of question[4]
That they do know my son, come you more nearer[5]
Than your particular demands will touch it.
Take you, as 'twere, some distant knowledge of him;
As thus, — " I know his father and his friends,
And in part him:" do you mark this, Reynaldo ?

Reynaldo. Ay, very well, my lord.

Polonius. " And in part him, but," you may say, " not well.
But if't be he I mean, he's very wild;
Addicted so and so:" and there put on him
What forgeries you please; marry, none so rank
As may dishonor him; take heed of that;
But, sir, such wanton, wild, and usual slips
As are companions noted and most known
To youth and liberty.

Reynaldo.   As gaming, my lord.

Polonius. Ay, or drinking, fencing, swearing, quarreling:
You may go so far.

Reynaldo. My lord, that would dishonor him.

Polonius. 'Faith, no; as you may season it in the charge.
You must not put another scandal on him,
That he is open to incontinency;
That's not my meaning: but breathe his faults so quaintly[6]
That they may seem the taints of liberty,
The flash and outbreak of a fiery mind,

---

[1] Danes.   [2] Live.

[3] Roundabout way.   [4] Conversation.

[5] Double comparatives, as " more nearer," are frequent with Shakespeare
and with all the writers of his age.

[6] " Breathe his faults so quaintly," i.e., speak of his faults with such art-
ful reservation.

A savageness in unreclaimed blood,
Of general assault.[1]

 Reynaldo.   But, my good lord—
 Polonius. Wherefore should you do this ?
 Reynaldo.   Ay, my lord,
I would know that.
 Polonius.   Marry, sir, here's my drift;
And, I believe, it is a fetch of warrant.[2]
You laying these slight sullies on my son,
As 'twere a thing a little soil'd i' the working,
Mark you,
Your party in converse', him you would sound,
Having ever seen in the prenominate [3] crimes
The youth you breathe of guilty, be assur'd
He closes with you in this consequence:
" Good sir," or so, or " friend," or " gentleman,"
According to the phrase or the addition [4]
Of man and country.
 Reynaldo.   Very good, my lord.
 Polonius. And then, sir, does he this—he does—what was I
about to say ? By the mass, I was about to say something:
where did I leave ?
 Reynaldo. At " closes in the consequence," at " friend or so,"
and " gentleman."
 Polonius. At " closes in the consequence," ay, marry;
He closes with you thus: " I know the gentleman;
I saw him yesterday, or t'other day,
Or then, or then; with such, or such; and, as you say,
There was he gaming; there o'ertook in's rouse;[5]
There falling out at tennis."

---

 [1] " A savageness," etc., i.e., a wildness common to all hot-blooded youths
not yet disciplined by the experience of life.
 [2] " Fetch of warrant," i.e., justifiable artifice.
 [3] Before-named.   [4] See Note 6, p. 42.
 [5] See Note 2, p. 31.

See you now;
Your bait of falsehood takes this carp[1] of truth:
And thus do we of wisdom and of reach,
With windlasses and with assays of bias,
By indirections find directions out:[2]
So by my former lecture and advice,
Shall you my son.   You have me, have you not?[3]

 Reynaldo. My lord, I have.

 Polonius.   God be wi' you; fare you well.

 Reynaldo. Good my lord!

 Polonius. Observe his inclination in[4] yourself.

 Reynaldo. I shall, my lord.

 Polonius. And let him ply his music.

 Reynaldo.   Well, my lord.

 Polonius. Farewell!   [*Exit Reynaldo.*

Enter OPHELIA.

      How now, Ophelia! what's the matter?

 Ophelia. O, my lord, my lord, I have been so affrighted!

 Polonius. With what, i' the name of God?

 Ophelia. My lord, as I was sewing in my closet,[5]
Lord Hamlet, with his doublet all unbrac'd;
No hat upon his head; his stockings foul'd,
Ungarter'd, and down-gyved[6] to his ankle;
Pale as his shirt; his knees knocking each other;

---

 [1] A kind of fish.

 [2] "With windlasses," etc.: "In Shakespeare's day, *windlace* (literally,
'a winding') was used to express taking a circuitous course, . . . making an
indirect advance, or, more colloquially, 'beating about the bush;' . . . and
in this sense it exactly harmonizes with the other phrase used by Polonius
to express the same thing, — 'assays of bias,' attempts in which, instead
of going straight to the object, we seek to reach it by a curved or winding
course." — *Edinburgh Review,* July, 1869.

 [3] "You have me," etc., i.e., you take my meaning; do you not?

 [4] For.   [5] Chamber.

 [6] Hanging like fetters about his ankles.

And with a look so piteous in purport'
As if he had been loosed out of hell
To speak of horrors,— he comes before me.

    Polonius. Mad for thy love?

    Ophelia.   My lord, I do not know;
But truly, I do fear it.

    Polonius.   What said he?

    Ophelia. He took me by the wrist, and held me hard;
Then goes he to the length of all his arm;
And, with his other hand thus o'er his brow,
He falls to such perusal of my face
As he would draw it.   Long stay'd he so;
At last, a little shaking of mine arm,
And thrice his head thus waving up and down,
He rais'd a sigh so piteous and profound
As it did seem to shatter all his bulk,[1]
And end his being.   That done, he lets me go:
And, with his head over his shoulder turn'd,
He seem'd to find his way without his eyes;
For out o' doors he went without their help,
And, to the last, bended their light on me.

    Polonius. Come, go with me: I will go seek the King.
This is the very ecstasy[2] of love,
Whose violent property fordoes[3] itself,
And leads the will to desperate undertakings
As oft as any passion under heaven
That does afflict our natures.   I am sorry.
What, have you given him any hard words of late?

    Ophelia. No, my good lord; but, as you did command,
I did repel his letters, and deni'd
His access to me.

    Polonius.   That hath made him mad.
I am sorry that with better heed and judgment

---

[1] Trunk; body.   [2] Madness.
[3] Destroys.

I had not quoted[1] him.   I fear'd he did but trifle,
And meant to wreck thee; but, beshrew my jealousy!
By Heaven, it is as proper to our age
To cast beyond ourselves in our opinions
As it is common for the younger sort
To lack discretion.   Come, go we to the King.
This must be known; which, being kept close, might move
More grief to hide than hate to utter love.[2]   [*Exeunt.*

Interval of 2 months.

SCENE II.   *A Room in the Castle.*

Enter KING, QUEEN, ROSENCRANTZ, GUILDENSTERN, *and* Attendants.

King. Welcome, dear Rosencrantz and Guildenstern!
Moreover[3] that we much did long to see you,
The need we have to use you did provoke
Our hasty sending.   Something have you heard
Of Hamlet's transformation; so call it,
Sith[4] nor[5] the exterior nor the inward man
Resembles that it was.   What it should be,
More than his father's death, that thus hath put him
So much from th' understanding of himself,
I cannot dream of.   I entreat you both,
That, being of so young days brought up with him,
And sith so neighbor'd to his youth and humor,
That you vouchsafe your rest[6] here in our court
Some little time: so by your companies
To draw him on to pleasures, and to gather,
So much as from occasion you may glean,

---

[1] Taken note of.

[2] "More grief to hide," etc., i.e., "This must be made known to the King; for (being kept secret) the hiding of Hamlet's love might occasion more mischief to us from him and the Queen than the uttering or revealing of it will occasion hate and resentment from Hamlet." — JOHNSON.

[3] Over and above the fact.   [4] Since.   [5] Neither.

[6] "Vouchsafe your rest," i.e., kindly grant us your company.

Whether aught, to us unknown, afflicts him thus,
That, open'd, lies within our remedy.

Queen. Good gentlemen, he hath much talk'd of you;
And sure I am two men there are not living
To whom he more adheres. If it will please you
To show us so much gentry [1] and good will
As to expend your time with us a while,
For the supply and profit of our hope, [2]
Your visitation shall receive such thanks
As fits a king's remembrance.

Rosencrantz. Both your Majesties
Might, by the sovereign power you have of us,
Put your dread pleasures more into command
Than to entreaty.

Guildenstern. But we both obey,
And here give up ourselves, in the full bent [3]
To lay our service freely at your feet,
To be commanded.

King. Thanks, Rosencrantz and gentle Guildenstern.

Queen. Thanks, Guildenstern and gentle Rosencrantz;
And I beseech you instantly to visit
My too much changed son. — Go, some of you,
And bring these gentlemen where Hamlet is.

Guildenstern. Heavens make our presence and our practices
Pleasant and helpful to him!

Queen. Ay, amen!
[*Exeunt Rosencrantz, Guildenstern, and some Attendants.*

Enter POLONIUS.

Polonius. Th' ambassadors from Norway, my good lord,
Are joyfully return'd.

---

[1] Complaisance.

[2] "For the supply," etc., i.e., that we may realize the hope which your coming has raised.

[3] Endeavor and inclination.

King. Thou still hast been the father of good news.

Polonius. Have I, my lord ?　I assure my good liege,
I hold my duty, as I hold my soul,
Both to my God and to my gracious King;
And I do think, or else this brain of mine
Hunts not the trail [1] of policy so sure
As it hath us'd to do, that I have found
The very cause of Hamlet's lunacy.

King. O, speak of that; that do I long to hear.

Polonius. Give first admittance to th' ambassadors;
My news shall be the fruit to that great feast.

King. Thyself do grace to them, and bring them in.

　　　　　　　　　　　　　　　　[Exit Polonius.

He tells me, my dear Gertrude, he hath found
The head and source of all your son's distemper.

Queen. I doubt it is no other but the main:
His father's death, and our o'erhasty marriage.

King. Well, we shall sift him.—

Reënter POLONIUS, *with* VOLTIMAND *and* CORNELIUS.

　　　　　　　　　　　Welcome, my good friends !
Say, Voltimand, what from our brother Norway ?

Voltimand. Most fair return of greetings and desires.
Upon our first,[2] he sent out to suppress
His nephew's levies; which to him appear'd
To be a preparation 'gainst the Polack;
But, better look'd into, he truly found
It was against your Highness: whereat griev'd,
That so his sickness, age, and impotence
Was falsely borne in hand,[3] sends out arrests
On Fortinbras; which he, in brief, obeys;

---

1 The "trail," in hunting, is the trace of the animal pursued by its scent.

2 "Upon our first," i.e., upon our first audience to make known our mission.

3 "Falsely borne in hand," i.e., imposed on.

Receives rebuke from Norway, and in fine
Makes vow before his uncle never more
To give the assay of arms [1] against your Majesty.
Whereon old Norway, overcome with joy,
Gives him three thousand crowns in annual fee,
And his commission to employ those soldiers,
So levied as before, against the Polack;
With an entreaty, herein further shown,   [*Giving a paper.*
That it might please you to give quiet pass
Through your dominions for this enterprise,
On such regards of safety and allowance [2]
As therein are set down.

    King.   It likes us well; [3]
And at our more consider'd time [4] we'll read,
Answer, and think upon this business.
Meantime we thank you for your well-took labor.
Go to your rest; at night we'll feast together:
Most welcome home!   [*Exeunt Voltimand and Cornelius.*
    Polonius.   This business is well ended.
My liege, and madam, to expostulate [5]
What majesty should be, what duty is,
Why day is day, night night, and time is time,
Were nothing but to waste night, day, and time.
Therefore, since brevity is the soul of wit, [6]
And tediousness the limbs and outward flourishes,
I will be brief.   Your noble son is mad:

---

[1] "To give the assay of arms," i.e., to make an armed attempt.

[2] "Regards of safety and allowance," i.e., conditions of security and permission.

[3] "It likes us well," i.e., we are well pleased with it.

[4] "At our more consider'd time," i.e., when we have more leisure for consideration.

[5] Discuss.

[6] Wisdom. "Wit was not, in Shakespeare's time, taken either for imagination or acuteness, or both together, but for understanding, for the faculty by which we apprehend and judge."—JOHNSON.

Mad call I it; for, to define true madness,
What is't but to be nothing else but mad?
But let that go.

    Queen.   More matter, with less art.
    Polonius. Madam, I swear I use no art at all.
That he is mad, 'tis true: 'tis true 'tis pity;
And pity 'tis 'tis true: a foolish figure;
But farewell it, for I will use no art.
Mad let us grant him, then; and now remains
That we find out the cause of this effect,
Or rather say, the cause of this defect,
For this effect defective comes by cause:
Thus it remains, and the remainder thus.
Perpend.[1]
I have a daughter,—have while she is mine,—
Who, in her duty and obedience, mark,
Hath given me this.   Now gather, and surmise.   [*Reads.*

   "To the celestial and my soul's idol, the most beautified Ophelia,"—

That's an ill phrase, a vile phrase; "beautified" is a vile phrase:
but you shall hear.   Thus: [*Reads.*

   "In her excellent white bosom, these," etc.

    Queen. Came this from Hamlet to her?
    Polonius. Good madam, stay a while; I will be faithful. [*Reads.*

           " Doubt thou the stars are fire;
              Doubt that the sun doth move;
              Doubt truth to be a liar;
              But never doubt I love.

  *" O dear Ophelia, I am ill at these numbers; I have not art to reckon
my groans: but that I love thee best, O most best, believe it.   Adieu.*
        " Thine evermore, most dear lady, whilst
               this machine[2] is to him, HAMLET."

---

[1] An affected, pedantic word signifying " ponder, consider."
[2] Body.

This, in obedience, hath my daughter shown me,
And more above,[1] hath his solicitings,
As they fell out by time, by means and place,
All given to mine ear.

  King.   But how hath she
Receiv'd his love?

  Polonius.   What do you think of me?

  King. As of a man faithful and honorable.

  Polonius. I would fain prove so. But what might you think,
When I had seen this hot love on the wing—
As I perceiv'd it, I must tell you that,
Before my daughter told me—what might you,
Or my dear Majesty, your Queen here, think,
If I had play'd the desk or tablebook,
Or given my heart a winking, mute and dumb,
Or look'd upon this love with idle sight;[2]
What might you think? No, I went round to work,[3]
And my young mistress thus I did bespeak:
"Lord Hamlet is a prince, out of thy star;[4]
This must not be:" and then I precepts gave her,
That she should lock herself from his resort,
Admit no messengers, receive no tokens.
Which done, she took the fruits of my advice;
And he, repulsed,—a short tale to make,—
Fell into a sadness, then into a fast,
Thence to a watch,[5] thence into a weakness,
Thence to a lightness, and by this declension,
Into the madness wherein now he raves,
And all we mourn for.

[1] " More above," i.e., more than this; moreover.
[2] "If I had play'd," etc., i.e., if I had been their confidant in this love affair, or had connived at it, or been negligent in observing it.
[3] " Round to work," i.e., to work without reserve; was outspoken.
[4] Sphere.
[5] Watchfulness; sleeplessness.

King.   Do you think 'tis this ?

Queen. It may be, very likely.

Polonius. Hath there been such a time — I'd fain know that —
That I have positively said, " 'Tis so,"
When it prov'd otherwise ?

King.   Not that I know.

Polonius. [*Pointing to his head and shoulder*] Take this from
       this, if this be otherwise.
If circumstances lead me, I will find
Where truth is hid, though it were hid indeed
Within the center.[1]

King.   How may we try it further ?

Polonius. You know, sometimes he walks for hours together
Here in the lobby.

Queen.   So he does indeed.

Polonius. At such a time I'll loose my daughter to him :
Be you and I behind an arras[2] then ;
Mark the encounter : if he love her not,
And be not from his reason fall'n thereon,
Let me be no assistant for a state,
But keep a farm and carters.

King.   We will try it.

Queen. But, look, where sadly the poor wretch[3] comes reading.

Polonius. Away, I do beseech you, both away.
I'll board[4] him presently.

                    [*Exeunt King, Queen, and Attendants.*

---

[1] That is, the center of the earth.

[2] Tapestry hangings, with which the principal rooms of houses were decorated. They were hung around the room, but, to avoid injury from the dampness of the walls, were not attached to them, but were suspended on frames set out from them ; so that " behind an arras " was a convenient hiding place. The name is from a town in France which had a large trade in these tapestries.

[3] " Poor wretch " was frequently used as a term of endearment, generally with a touch of pity in it.   [4] Accost.

Enter HAMLET, *reading.*

O, give me leave:
How does my good Lord Hamlet ?

Hamlet. Well, God-a-mercy.

Polonius. Do you know me, my lord ?

Hamlet. Excellent well; you're a fishmonger.

Polonius. Not I, my lord.

Hamlet. Then I would you were so honest a man.

Polonius. Honest, my lord !

Hamlet. Ay, sir; to be honest, as this world goes, is to be one man pick'd out of ten thousand.

Polonius. That's very true, my lord.

Hamlet. "For if the sun breed maggots in a dead dog, being a god, kissing carrion "— Have you a daughter ?

Polonius. I have, my lord. [*Aside*] Still harping on my daughter: yet he knew me not at first; he said I was a fishmonger. He is far gone, far gone: and truly in my youth I suffer'd much extremity for love; very near this. I'll speak to him again. — What do you read, my lord ?

Hamlet. Words, words, words.

Polonius. What is the matter, my lord ?

Hamlet. Between who ?[1]

Polonius. I mean, the matter that you read, my lord.

Hamlet. Slanders, sir; for the satirical rogue says here that old men have gray beards, that their faces are wrinkl'd, their eyes purging thick amber and plum-tree gum, and that they have a plentiful lack of wit, together with most weak hams: all which, sir, though I most powerfully and potently believe, yet I hold it not honesty to have it thus set down; for yourself, sir, should be old as I am, if like a crab you could go backward.

Polonius. [*Aside*] Though this be madness, yet there is method in't. — Will you walk out of the air, my lord ?

Hamlet. Into my grave.

Polonius. Indeed, that is out o' the air. [*Aside*] How preg-

---

1 Whom.

nant[1] sometimes his replies are! a happiness that often madness
hits on, which reason and sanity could not so prosperously be
deliver'd of.   I will leave him, and suddenly contrive the means
of meeting between him and my daughter. — My honorable lord,
I will most humbly take my leave of you.

Hamlet. You cannot, sir, take from me anything that I will more
willingly part withal; except my life, except my life, except my life.

Polonius. Fare you well, my lord.

Hamlet. These tedious old fools !

Enter ROSENCRANTZ *and* GUILDENSTERN.

Polonius. You go to seek the Lord Hamlet; there he is.

Rosencrantz. [*To Polonius*] God save you, sir ! [*Exit Polonius.*

Guildenstern. My honor'd lord !

Rosencrantz. My most dear lord !

Hamlet. My excellent good friends !   How dost thou, Guildenstern ?   Ah, Rosencrantz !   Good lads, how do you both ?

Rosencrantz. As the indifferent[2] children of the earth.

Guildenstern. Happy, in that we are not over happy;
On Fortune's cap we are not the very button.

Hamlet. Nor the soles of her shoe ?

Rosencrantz. Neither, my lord.

Hamlet. What's the news ?

Rosencrantz. None, my lord, but that the world's grown honest.

Hamlet. Then is doomsday near; but your news is not true.
Let me question more in particular : what have you, my good
friends, deserv'd at the hands of Fortune, that she sends you to
prison hither ?

Guildenstern. Prison, my lord !

Hamlet. Denmark's a prison.

Rosencrantz. Then is the world one.

Hamlet. A goodly one; in which there are many confines,[3]
wards,[4] and dungeons, Denmark being one o' the worst.

---

[1] Apt.   [2] Average.

[3] Places of confinement.   [4] Cells for safe keeping.

Rosencrantz. We think not so, my lord.

Hamlet. Why, then, 'tis none to you; for there is nothing either good or bad, but thinking makes it so. To me it is a prison.

Rosencrantz. Why, then, your ambition makes it one; 'tis too narrow for your mind.

Hamlet. O God, I could be bounded in a nutshell and count myself a king of infinite space, were it not that I have bad dreams.

Guildenstern. Which dreams indeed are ambition, for the very substance of the ambitious is merely the shadow of a dream.

Hamlet. A dream itself is but a shadow.

Rosencrantz. Truly; and I hold ambition of so airy and light a quality that it is but a shadow's shadow.

Hamlet. Then are our beggars bodies, and our monarchs and outstretch'd heroes the beggars' shadows. Shall we to the court? for, by my fay,[1] I cannot reason.

Rosencrantz.
Guildenstern. } We'll wait upon you.

Hamlet. No such matter: I will not sort[2] you with the rest of my servants, for, to speak to you like an honest man, I am most dreadfully attended. But, in the beaten way of friendship, what make you[3] at Elsinore?

Rosencrantz. To visit you, my lord; no other occasion.[4]

Hamlet. Beggar that I am, I am even poor in thanks; but I thank you: and sure, dear friends, my thanks are too dear a halfpenny. Were you not sent for? Is it your own inclining? Is it a free visitation? Come, deal justly with me: come, come; nay, speak.

Guildenstern. What should we say, my lord?

Hamlet. Why, anything, but to the purpose. You were sent for; and there is a kind of confession in your looks which your modesties have not craft enough to color.[5] I know the good King and Queen have sent for you.

---

1 Faith.   2 Class.   3 See Note 4, p. 32.
4 Motive.   5 Cover.

Rosencrantz. To what end, my lord?

Hamlet. That you must teach me. But let me conjure you, by the rights of our fellowship, by the consonancy [1] of our youth, by the obligation of our ever-preserved love, and by what more dear a better proposer could charge you withal, be even and direct with me, whether you were sent for, or no?

Rosencrantz. [*Aside to Guildenstern*] What say you?

Hamlet. [*Aside*] Nay, then, I have an eye of you.—If you love me, hold not off.

Guildenstern. My lord, we were sent for.

Hamlet. I will tell you why; so shall my anticipation prevent your discovery, and your secrecy to the King and Queen molt [2] no feather. I have of late—but wherefore I know not—lost all my mirth, forgone all custom of exercises; and indeed it goes so heavily with my disposition that this goodly frame, the earth, seems to me a sterile promontory; this most excellent canopy, the air, look you, this brave o'erhanging firmament, this majestical roof fretted [3] with golden fire, why, it appears no other thing to me than a foul and pestilent congregation of vapors. What a piece of work is man! how noble in reason! how infinite in faculty! in form and moving how express [4] and admirable! in action how like an angel! in apprehension how like a god! the beauty of the world! the paragon of animals! [5] And yet, to me, what is this quintessence of dust? man delights not me: no, nor woman neither, though by your smiling you seem to say so.

Rosencrantz. My lord, there was no such stuff in my thoughts.

Hamlet. Why did you laugh, then, when I said, "man delights not me"?

Rosencrantz. To think, my lord, if you delight not in man, what lenten entertainment [6] the players shall receive from you.

[1] Harmonious intimacy.

[2] Lose, or shed.   [3] Ornamented.

[4] Exact; fitted to its purpose.

[5] "Paragon of animals," i.e., without a peer among animals.

[6] "Lenten entertainment," i.e., scanty welcome.

We coted [1] them on the way; and hither are they coming, to offer you service.

Hamlet. He that plays the king shall be welcome; his Majesty shall have tribute of me; the adventurous knight shall use his foil and target; the lover shall not sigh gratis; the humorous man shall end his part in peace; the clown shall make those laugh whose lungs are tickle o' the sere; [2] and the lady shall say her mind freely, or the blank verse shall halt for't. What players are they?

Rosencrantz. Even those you were wont to take delight in, the tragedians of the city.

Hamlet. How chances it they travel? their residence, both in reputation and profit, was better both ways.

Rosencrantz. I think their inhibition comes by the means of the late innovation. [3]

Hamlet. Do they hold the same estimation they did when I was in the city? Are they so follow'd?

Rosencrantz. No, indeed, are they not.

Hamlet. How comes it? Do they grow rusty?

Rosencrantz. Nay, their endeavor keeps in the wonted pace. But there is, sir, an aerie [4] of children, little eyases, [5] that cry out on the top of question, [6] and are most tyrannically [7] clapped for't. These are now the fashion, and so berattle the common stages —so they call them—that many wearing rapiers are afraid of goose quills, and dare scarce come thither. [8]

---

[1] Overtook and passed.

[2] " Make those laugh," etc., i.e., make those laugh who are easily excited to mirth. The " sere," or " sear," is the catch of a gunlock.

[3] Collier (as quoted by Furness) remarks: " This passage [inhibition comes, etc.] probably refers to the limiting of public performances [in London] to the two theaters, the Globe and the Fortune, in 1600 and 1601. The players by a ' late innovation ' were ' inhibited,' or forbidden to act in or near the city, and therefore traveled, or ' strolled,' into the country."

[4] A brood, or nest.   [5] Young hawks; figuratively, unfledged novices.

[6] " Cry out," etc., i.e., assert superiority; proclaim themselves superior.

[7] Vehemently.

[8] " These are now the fashion," etc., i.e., " These young hawks make such

Hamlet. What, are they children? who maintains 'em? how are they escoted?[1] Will they pursue the quality[2] no longer than they can sing? will they not say afterwards, if they should grow themselves to common players—as it is most like, if their means are no better—their writers do them wrong, to make them exclaim against their own succession?

Rosencrantz. 'Faith, there has been much to do on both sides; and the nation holds it no sin to tarre[3] them to controversy. There was, for a while, no money bid for argument,[4] unless the poet and the player went to cuffs in the question.

Hamlet. Is't possible?

Guildenstern. O, there has been much throwing about of brains.

Hamlet. Do the boys carry it away?

Rosencrantz. Ay, that they do, my lord; Hercules and his load[5] too.

Hamlet. It is not very strange; for mine uncle is King of Denmark, and those that would make mows at him while my father liv'd give twenty, forty, fifty, an hundred ducats apiece for his picture in little. 'Sblood, there is something in this more than natural, if philosophy could find it out.

　　　　　　　　　　　　　　[*Flourish of trumpets within.*

Guildenstern. There are the players.

Hamlet. Gentlemen, you are welcome to Elsinore. Your hands, come then. The appurtenance of welcome is fashion

---

a noise on the common stage, that the dramatists, whose wit is as keen as a rapier, are afraid to encounter these chits who fight, as it were, with a goose quill."—REV. C. E. MOBERLY.　　　[1] Paid.

　　[2] Profession, or calling.　　　[3] Urge; incite.　　　[4] Plot of a play.

　　[5] "Hercules and his load:" we read in classic mythology that Atlas, one of the Titans, having assisted the giants in their war against the gods, Jupiter condemned him to bear the heavens upon his shoulders; and it is further fabled that Hercules (see Note 3, p. 32), in return for a favor granted him by Atlas, relieved the Titan of his burden. (See GUERBER's *Myths of Gerece and Rome*, p. 228.) Possibly there is an allusion in the text to the Globe Theater, in which Shakespeare was interested. Its sign was Hercules bearing a globe.

and ceremony: let me comply with you in this garb,[1] lest my extent to the players, which, I tell you, must show fairly outward, should more appear like entertainment than yours. You are welcome; but my uncle-father and aunt-mother are deceiv'd.

Guildenstern. In what, my dear lord?

Hamlet. I am but mad north-northwest: when the wind is southerly, I know a hawk from a handsaw.[2]

Reënter POLONIUS.

Polonius. Well be with you, gentlemen!

Hamlet. Hark you, Guildenstern; — and you too; — at each ear a hearer: that great baby you see there is not yet out of his swaddling clouts.

Rosencrantz. Happily[3] he's the second time come to them; for they say an old man is twice a child.

Hamlet. I will prophesy he comes to tell me of the players; mark it. You say right, sir: o' Monday morning; 'twas so indeed.

Polonius. My lord, I have news to tell you.

Hamlet. My lord, I have news to tell you. When Roscius was an actor in Rome, —

Polonius. The actors are come hither, my lord.

Hamlet. Buz, buz![4]

Polonius. Upon mine honor, —

Hamlet. Then came each actor on his ass, —

Polonius. The best actors in the world, either for tragedy, comedy, history, pastoral, pastoral-comical, historical-pastoral, tragical-historical, tragical-comical-historical-pastoral, scene individable, or poem unlimited: Seneca cannot be too heavy, nor Plautus[5]

[1] "Let me comply with you in this garb," i.e., let my welcome to you have this outward formality.

[2] "Know a hawk from a handsaw" (originally "hernshaw," a heron) was in old proverbial expression in Shakespeare's time.

[3] Haply; perhaps.   [4] Fudge; idle talk.

[5] "Seneca," etc.: "The tragedies of Seneca were translated into Eng-

too light. For the law of writ and the liberty,[1] these are the only men.

Hamlet. O Jephthah, judge of Israel,[2] what a treasure hadst thou !

Polonius. What a treasure had he, my lord ?

Hamlet. Why,

> " *One fair daughter, and no more,*
>   *The which he loved passing well.*"

Polonius. [*Aside*] Still on my daughter.

Hamlet. Am I not i' the right, old Jephthah ?

Polonius. If you call me Jephthah, my lord, I have a daughter that I love passing well.

Hamlet. Nay, that follows not.

Polonius. What follows, then, my lord ?

Hamlet. Why,

> "*As by lot, God wot,*"

and then, you know,

> " *It came to pass, as most like it was,*"—

the first row [3] of the pious chanson [4] will show you more; for look, where my abridgment [5] comes.—

Enter four or five Players.

You are welcome, masters; welcome, all. I am glad to see thee well. Welcome, good friends.—O, my old friend ! thy face is

lish . . . and published in 1581. One comedy of Plautus . . . was likewise translated and published in 1565."—WARTON.

1 " Law of writ," etc., i.e., adhering to their text, or extemporizing when necessary.

2 For the story of Jephthah and his daughter, see Judg. xi. 30–40. Hamlet quotes from an old ballad founded on this story.   3 Stanza.

4 " Pious chanson," i.e., a kind of Christmas carol containing some scriptural history thrown into loose rhymes, and sung about the streets by common people when they went at that season to solicit alms.

5 Further along in this scene Hamlet speaks of the players as " the abstracts and brief chronicles of the time." (See p. 76.)

valanc'd [1] since I saw thee last: com'st thou to beard me in Denmark?—What, my young lady and mistress! By'r lady, your ladyship is nearer to heaven than when I saw you last, by the altitude of a chopine.[2] Pray God, your voice, like a piece of uncurrent gold, be not crack'd [3] within the ring.—Masters, you are all welcome. We'll e'en to't like French falconers, fly at anything we see: we'll have a speech straight. Come, give us a taste of your quality; come, a passionate speech.

First Player. What speech, my lord?

Hamlet. I heard thee speak me a speech once, but it was never acted; or, if it was, not above once, for the play, I remember, pleas'd not the million; 'twas caviare [4] to the general: [5] but it was—as I receiv'd it, and others, whose judgments in such matters cried in the top of mine [6]—an excellent play, well digested in the scenes, set down with as much modesty as cunning. I remember, one said there were no sallets in the lines to make the matter savory, nor no matter in the phrase that might indict [7] the author of affection,[8] but call'd it an honest method, as wholesome as sweet, and by very much more handsome than fine.

---

[1] Fringed, referring here to the player's beard.

[2] Coryat in his Crudities (1611), quoted in a note in Johnson and Steevens's Shakespeare (edition 1785), describes the "chopine," which he calls "chapiney." He says, "There is one thing used by the Venetian women . . . which is so common that no woman whatsoever goeth without it, either in her house or abroad,—a thing made of wood covered with leather of sundry colors, some white, some redde, some yellow. It is called a chapiney, which they wear under their shoes. There are many of these chapineys of great height, . . . which maketh many of these women, which are very short, seeme much taller than the tallest women we have in England."

[3] Changed too much for use. This is said to the youth who acted women's parts. There were no women on the stage in England before the reign of Charles II.

[4] A Russian condiment prepared from the roes of sturgeon and other fish. It needed an acquired taste to relish it.

[5] People generally.

[6] See Note 6, p. 68.

[7] Accuse.   [8] Affectation.

One speech in it I chiefly lov'd : 'twas Æneas' tale to Dido,[1] and thereabout of it especially, where he speaks of Priam's slaughter. If it live in your memory, begin at this line : let me see, let me see —

> "*The rugged Pyrrhus, like the Hyrcanian beast,*"[2] —

it is not so : it begins with Pyrrhus.

> "*The rugged Pyrrhus, he whose sable arms,*
> *Black as his purpose, did the night resemble*
> *When he lay couched in the ominous horse,*[3]
> *Hath now this dread and black complexion smear'd*
> *With heraldry*[4] *more dismal ; head to foot*
> *Now is he total gules ;*[5] *horridly trick'd*[6]
> *With blood of fathers, mothers, daughters, sons,*
> *Bak'd and impasted with the parching streets,*
> *That lend a tyrannous and damned light*
> *To their vile murders.   Roasted in wrath and fire,*
> *And thus o'er-sized*[7] *with coagulate gore,*

[1] " Æneas' tale to Dido," as related in Virgil's Æneid, is that Æneas, a Trojan prince, after the destruction of Troy by the Greeks, set sail with his followers, intending to found a colony in Italy.   His vessels were driven by a storm on to the coast of Africa, where he was hospitably welcomed and entertained by Dido, Queen of Carthage, whose heart he quite won by his manly bearing and his eloquent description of incidents in the siege of Troy. According to the poem, Priam was the King of Troy, Hecuba was his Queen, and Pyrrhus was a general of the Grecian forces.

[2] " Hyrcanian beast," i.e., the tiger.   Hyrcania was a name given by the ancients to a territory of uncertain extent lying south of the Caspian Sea.   It was supposed by old writers to be a land of tigers.

[3] " Ominous horse," i.e., an enormous wooden horse constructed by the Greeks, which, by an artifice, the Trojans were persuaded to bring within their walls.   In the night a band of Greeks concealed in it released themselves, opened the gates of the town to the Grecian warriors waiting without, who, rushing in, pillaged and burned the city.

[4] " Smear'd with heraldry," i.e., painted with colors used in heraldic devices.

[5] Red.

[6] Besmeared.

[7] " Size," or " sizing," is a kind of glue.

> *With eyes like carbuncles,*[1] *the hellish Pyrrhus*
> *Old grandsire Priam seeks."*

So, proceed you.

Polonius. 'Fore God, my lord, well spoken, with good accent and good discretion.

> *First Player.*   *"Anon he finds him*
> *Striking too short at Greeks: his an'tique sword,*
> *Rebellious to his arm, lies where it falls,*
> *Repugnant to command.   Unequal match'd,*
> *Pyrrhus at Priam drives; in rage strikes wide;*
> *But with the whiff and wind of his fell sword*
> *The unnerved father falls.   Then senseless Ilium,*[2]
> *Seeming to feel this blow, with flaming top*
> *Stoops to his base, and with a hideous crash*
> *Takes prisoner Pyrrhus' ear: for, lo! his sword,*
> *Which was declining on the milky head*
> *Of reverend Priam, seem'd i' the air to stick:*
> *So, as a painted tyrant, Pyrrhus stood,*
> *And like a neutral to his will and matter,*
> *Did nothing.*
> *But, as we often see, against some storm,*
> *A silence in the heavens, the rack*[3] *stand still,*
> *The bold winds speechless, and the orb below*
> *As hush as death, anon the dreadful thunder*
> *Doth rend the region;*[4] *so, after Pyrrhus' pause,*
> *Aroused vengeance sets him new awork;*
> *And never did the Cyclops'*[5] *hammers fall*
> *On Mars's*[6] *armor forg'd for proof eterne*[7]

---

[1] " Eyes like carbuncles," i.e., eyes blood-red as carbuncles.

[2] Priam, the King of Ilium (Troy).

[3] Clouds.

[4] The air.

[5] " The Cyclops " were Titans of gigantic stature, having but one eye each, — a large round one, — which flamed fiercely from the middle of the forehead. They assisted Vulcan, who forged Jupiter's thunderbolts, and made armor for the gods and heroes of antiquity.

[6] The god of war of classic mythology.

[7] " Proof eterne," i.e., absolutely proof against all assaults.

With less remorse [1] than Pyrrhus' bleeding sword
Now falls on Priam.
Out, out, inconstant Fortune! All you gods,
In general synod, take away her power;
Break all the spokes and fellies [2] from her wheel,
And bowl the round nave [3] down the hill of heaven,
As low as to the fiends!"

Polonius. This is too long.

Hamlet. It shall to the barber's, with your beard. — Prithee, say on: — he's for a jig, or a tale of bawdry, or he sleeps. — Say on; come to Hecuba.

First Player. *"But who, O, who had seen the mobled [4] Queen"* —

Hamlet. "The mobled Queen?"

Polonius. That's good; "mobled Queen" is good.

First Player. *"Run barefoot up and down, threat'ning the flames*
With bisson rheum; [5] a clout upon that head
Where late the diadem stood, and for a robe,
About her lank and all o'er-teemed loins,
A blanket, in the alarm of fear caught up;
Who this had seen, with tongue in venom steep'd,
'Gainst Fortune's state would treason have pronounc'd:
But if the gods themselves did see her then,
When she saw Pyrrhus make malicious sport
In mincing with his sword her husband's limbs,
The instant burst of clamor that she made,
Unless things mortal move them not at all,
Would have made milch [6] the burning eyes of heaven,
And passion [7] in the gods."

Polonius. Look, whether he has not turn'd his color, and has tears in's eyes. Pray you, no more.

---

[1] Compassion.
[2] Pieces of wood on which the tire that binds the wheel is laid.
[3] Hub.   [4] Muffled.
[5] Blinding tears.   [6] Moist.   [7] Pity.

Hamlet. 'Tis well; I'll have thee speak out the rest soon.—
Good my lord, will you see the players well bestow'd? Do you
hear, let them be well us'd; for they are the abstracts and brief
chronicles of the time: after your death you were better have a
bad epitaph than their ill report while you live.

Polonius. My lord, I will use them according to their desert.

Hamlet. 'Od's bodykins, man, much better! Use every man
after his desert, and who should 'scape whipping? Use them
after your own honor and dignity: the less they deserve, the more
merit is in your bounty. Take them in.

Polonius. Come, sirs.

Hamlet. Follow him, friends: we'll hear a play to-morrow.
[*Exit Polonius with all the Players but the First.*] Dost thou
hear me, old friend? Can you play the Murder of Gonzago?

First Player. Ay, my lord.

Hamlet. We'll ha't to-morrow night. You could, for a need,
study[1] a speech of some dozen or sixteen lines which I would
set down and insert in't, could you not?

First Player. Ay, my lord.

Hamlet. Very well. Follow that lord; and look you mock
him not. [*Exit First Player.*] My good friends, I'll leave you
till night: you are welcome to Elsinore.

Rosencrantz. Good my lord!

Hamlet. Ay, so, God be wi'[2] ye.

[*Exeunt Rosencrantz and Guildenstern.*
Now I am alone.

O, what a rogue and peasant slave am I!
Is it not monstrous that this player here,
But in a fiction, in a dream of passion,
Could force his soul so to his own conceit[3]
That from her working all his visage wann'd,

---

[1] Commit to memory.

[2] "God be wi' you" is a step, in the abbreviation of "God be with you,"
to our "good-by."

[3] The idea he had conceived.

Tears in his eyes, distraction in's aspect',
A broken voice, and his whole function [1] suiting
With forms to his conceit?   And all for nothing!
For Hecuba!
What's Hecuba to him, or he to Hecuba,
That he should weep for her?   What would he do,
Had he the motive and the cue [2] for passion
That I have?   He would drown the stage with tears,
And cleave the general ear with horrid speech;
Make mad the guilty, and appall the free,
Confound the ignorant, and amaze indeed
The very faculties of eyes and ears.
Yet I,
A dull and muddy-mettled rascal, peak,[3]
Like John-a-dreams,[4] unpregnant [5] of my cause,
And can say nothing; no, not for a king,
Upon whose property and most dear life
A damn'd defeat [6] was made.   Am I a coward?
Who calls me villain? breaks my pate across?
Plucks off my beard, and blows it in my face?
Tweaks me by the nose? gives me the lie i' the throat,
As deep as to the lungs?   Who does me this?
Ha!
'Swounds, I should take it! for it cannot be
But I am pigeon-liver'd, and lack gall

---

1 Mental and bodily energy.

2 Prompting; technically, among players, the last word of the preceding speech prefixed to the speech of an actor to let him know that he is to come on the stage.

3 Mope.

4 "'John-a-dreams' (i.e., 'of dreams') means only 'John the dreamer,' a nickname, I suppose, for any ignorant, silly fellow. Thus the puppet formerly thrown at during the season of Lent was called 'Jack-a-lent,' and the ignis fatuus, 'Jack-a-lantern.'"—JOHNSON and STEEVENS: *Shakespeare* (edition 1785).

5 Incapable.   6 Ruin.

To make oppression bitter, or ere this
I should have fatted all the region kites
With this slave's offal.   Bloody, bawdy villain !
Remorseless, treacherous, lecherous, kindless [1] villain !
O, vengeance !
Why, what an ass am I !   This is most brave,
That I, the son of a dear father murder'd,
Prompted to my revenge by heaven and hell,
Must, like a wench, unpack my heart with words,
And fall acursing, like a very drab,
A scullion !
Fie upon't ! foh !   About, my brain !   I have heard
That guilty creatures sitting at a play
Have by the very cunning of the scene
Been struck so to the soul, that presently
They have proclaim'd their malefactions; [2]
For murder, though it have no tongue, will speak
With most miraculous organ.   I'll have these players
Play something like the murder of my father,
Before mine uncle.   I'll observe his looks;
I'll tent [3] him to the quick : if he but blench, [4]
I know my course.   The spirit that I have seen
May be the devil ; and the devil hath power
To assume a pleasing shape ; yea, and perhaps
Out of my weakness and my melancholy,
As he is very potent with such spirits,
Abuses me to damn me. [5]   I'll have grounds
More relative [6] than this : the play's the thing
Wherein I'll catch the conscience of the King.   [Exit.

1 Void of natural feeling.
2 Evil deeds.
3 Probe.
4 Shrink with fear.
5 " Abuses me to damn me," i.e., misleads me to my ruin.
6 To the purpose.

ACT III.

Scene I.   *A Room in the Castle.*

Enter King, Queen, Polonius, Ophelia, Rosencrantz, *and*
Guildenstern.

King. And can you, by no drift of circumstance,[1]
Get from him why he puts on this confusion,
Grating so harshly all his days of quiet
With turbulent and dangerous lunacy ?

Rosencrantz. He does confess he feels himself distracted ;
But from what cause he will by no means speak.

Guildenstern. Nor do we find him forward to be sounded,
But with a crafty madness keeps aloof
When we would bring him on to some confession
Of his true state.

Queen.   Did he receive you well ?

Rosencrantz. Most like a gentleman.

Guildenstern. But with much forcing of his disposition.

Rosencrantz. Niggard of question, but of our demands
Most free in his reply.

Queen.   Did you assay [2] him
To any pastime ?

Rosencrantz. Madam, it so fell out that certain players
We o'erraught on the way : of these we told him ;
And there did seem in him a kind of joy
To hear of it.   They are about the court,
And, as I think, they have already order
This night to play before him.

Polonius.   'Tis most true ;
And he beseech'd me to entreat your Majesties
To hear and see the matter.

King. With all my heart ; and it doth much content me

---

[1] " Drift of circumstance," i.e., indirect way.   [2] Tempt.

To hear him so inclin'd.
Good gentlemen, give him a further edge,
And drive his purpose on to these delights.

   Rosencrantz. We shall, my lord.

                    [*Exeunt Rosencrantz and Guildenstern.*

   King.   Sweet Gertrude, leave us too;
For we have closely sent for Hamlet hither,
That he, as 'twere by accident, may here
Affront [1] Ophelia.
Her father and myself, lawful espials,
Will so bestow ourselves, that seeing, unseen,
We may of their encounter frankly judge,
And gather by him, as he is behav'd,
If't be the affliction of his love, or no,
That thus he suffers for.

   Queen.   I shall obey you.—
And for your part, Ophelia, I do wish
That your good beauties be the happy cause
Of Hamlet's wildness: [2] so shall I hope your virtues
Will bring him to his wonted way again,
To both your honors.

   Ophelia.   Madam, I wish it may. [*Exit Queen.*

   Polonius. Ophelia, walk you here.—Gracious, [3] so please you,
We will bestow ourselves. [*To Ophelia.*] Read on this book;
That show of such an exercise may color
Your loneliness. We are oft to blame in this,—
'Tis too much prov'd,—that with devotion's visage
And pious action we do sugar o'er
The devil himself.

   King.   [*Aside*] O, 'tis too true!
How smart a lash that speech doth give my conscience!
The harlot's cheek, beauti'd with plast'ring art,

---

1 Confront; meet.
2 Eccentricities.
3 Addressed to the King.

Is not more ugly to [1] the thing that helps it
Than is my deed to my most painted [2] word.
O heavy burthen!

   Polonius. I hear him coming: let's withdraw, my lord.

                         [*Exeunt King and Polonius.*

Enter HAMLET.

   Hamlet. To be, or not to be; that is the question:
Whether 'tis nobler in the mind to suffer
The slings and arrows of outrageous fortune,
Or to take arms against a sea of troubles,
And by opposing end them? To die,—to sleep,—
No more; and by a sleep to say we end
The heartache and the thousand natural shocks
That flesh is heir to,—'tis a consummation
Devoutly to be wish'd. To die,—to sleep,—
To sleep! perchance to dream! ay, there's the rub;
For in that sleep of death what dreams may come,
When we have shuffled off this mortal coil,[3]
Must give us pause. There's the respect [4]
That makes calamity of so long life;
For who would bear the whips and scorns of time,
The oppressor's wrong, the proud man's contumely,
The pangs of despis'd love, the law's delay,
The insolence of office, and the spurns
That patient merit of the unworthy takes,
When he himself might his quietus [5] make
With a bare bodkin? [6] who would fardels [7] bear,

---

   1 Compared to.

   2 Disguised or hypocritical.

   3 " Mortal coil," i.e., the worry and turmoil of this life.

   4 Consideration.

   5 Release. " Quietus " is a law term for the full settlement and satisfaction of an account.

   6 The old name for a small dagger.

   7 Burdens.

To grunt and sweat under a weary life,
But that the dread of something after death,
The undiscover'd country from whose bourn [1]
No traveler returns, puzzles the will,
And makes us rather bear those ills we have
Than fly to others that we know not of ?
Thus conscience does make cowards of us all;
And thus the native hue of resolution
Is sickli'd o'er with the pale cast of thought,
And enterprises of great pith and moment [2]
With this regard their currents turn awry,
And lose the name of action.— Soft you now !
The fair Ophelia ! — Nymph, in thy orisons
Be all my sins remember'd.

    Ophelia.   Good my lord,
How does your honor for this many a day ?

    Hamlet. I humbly thank you; well, well, well.

    Ophelia. My lord, I have remembrances of yours,
That I have longed long to redeliver.
I pray you, now receive them.

    Hamlet.   No, not I;
I never gave you aught.

    Ophelia. My honor'd lord, I know right well you did;
And with them, words of so sweet breath compos'd
As made the things more rich : their perfume lost,
Take these again; for to the noble mind
Rich gifts wax [3] poor when givers prove unkind.
There, my lord.

    Hamlet. Ha, ha ! are you honest ?

    Ophelia. My lord ?

    Hamlet. Are you fair ?

    Ophelia. What means your lordship ?

---

[1] Confines ; boundary.
[2] " Of great pith and moment," i.e., full of matter of vital importance.
[3] Grow.

Hamlet. That if you be honest and fair, your honesty should admit no discourse to [1] your beauty.

Ophelia. Could beauty, my lord, have better commerce [2] than with honesty?

Hamlet. Ay, truly; for the power of beauty will sooner transform honesty from what it is to a bawd than the force of honesty can translate beauty into his [3] likeness: this was sometime a paradox, but now the time gives it proof. I did love you once.

Ophelia. Indeed, my lord, you made me believe so.

Hamlet. You should not have believ'd me; for virtue cannot so inoculate our old stock, but we shall relish of it. I loved you not.

Ophelia. I was the more deceived.

Hamlet. Get thee to a nunnery: why wouldst thou marry with a sinner? I am myself indifferent honest; [4] but yet I could accuse me of such things that it were better my mother had not borne me. I am very proud, revengeful, ambitious, with more offenses at my beck [5] than I have thoughts to put them in, imagination to give them shape, or time to act them in. What should such fellows as I do crawling between earth and heaven? We are arrant knaves, all; believe none of us. Go thy ways to a nunnery. Where's your father?

Ophelia. At home, my lord.

Hamlet. Let the doors be shut upon him, that he may play the fool nowhere but in's own house. Farewell.

Ophelia. O, help him, you sweet heavens!

Hamlet. If thou dost marry, I'll give thee this plague for thy dowry: be thou as chaste as ice, as pure as snow, thou shalt not escape calumny. Get thee to a nunnery, go; farewell. Or, if thou wilt needs marry, marry a fool; for wise men know well enough what monsters you make of them. To a nunnery, go, and quickly too. Farewell.

---

1 " Discourse to," i.e., intercourse with.

2 Conversation. 3 See Note 1, p. 39.

4 " Indifferent honest," i.e., of average honesty. 5 Call.

Ophelia. O heavenly powers, restore him !

Hamlet. I have heard of your paintings too, well enough ; God has given you one face, and you make yourselves another : you jig, you amble, and you lisp, and nickname God's creatures, and make your wantonness your ignorance.   Go to, I'll no more on't ; it hath made me mad.   I say, we will have no more mar- riages : those that are married already, all but one, shall live ; the rest shall keep as they are.   To a nunnery, go.   [*Exit.*

Ophelia. O, what a noble mind is here o'erthrown !
The courtier's, scholar's, soldier's, eye, tongue, sword ;
The expectancy and rose of the fair State,
The glass of fashion and the mold of form,[1]
The observ'd of all observers, quite, quite down !
And I, of ladies most deject and wretched,
That suck'd the honey of his music vows,
Now see that noble and most sovereign reason,
Like sweet bells jangled, out of tune and harsh ;
That unmatch'd form and feature of blown youth[2]
Blasted with ecstasy.   O, woe is me,
To have seen what I have seen, see what I see !

Reënter KING *and* POLONIUS.

King. Love ! his affections do not that way tend ;
Nor what he spake, though it lack'd form a little,
Was not like madness.   There's something in his soul,
O'er which his melancholy sits on brood ;[3]
And I do doubt the hatch and the disclose
Will be some danger ; which for to prevent,
I have in quick determination
Thus set it down : he shall with speed to England
For the demand of our neglected tribute.

[1] " The glass of fashion," etc., i.e., " the model by whom all endeavored to form themselves." — JOHNSON.

[2] " Blown youth," i.e., in the bloom of youth.

[3] " Sits on brood," i.e., sits brooding, as the bird on its eggs.

Haply the seas and countries different
With variable objects shall expel
This something-settled matter in his heart,
Whereon his brains still beating puts him thus
From fashion of himself.[1]   What think you on't ?

  Polonius. It shall do well; but yet do I believe
The origin and commencement of his grief
Sprung from neglected love.— How now, Ophelia !
You need not tell us what Lord Hamlet said;
We heard it all.— My lord, do as you please;
But, if you hold it fit, after the play
Let his Queen-mother all alone entreat him
To show his grief: let her be round with him;
And I'll be plac'd, so please you, in the ear
Of all their conference.   If she find him not,[2]
To England send him, or confine him where
Your wisdom best shall think.

  King.   It shall be so.
Madness in great ones must not unwatch'd go.   [*Exeunt.*

SCENE II.   *A Hall in the Castle.*

Enter HAMLET *and* Players.

  Hamlet. Speak the speech, I pray you, as I pronounc'd it to you, trippingly on the tongue; but if you mouth it, as many of your players do, I had as lief the town-crier spoke my lines. Nor do not saw the air too much with your hand, thus, but use all gently; for in the very torrent, tempest, and, as I may say, the whirlwind of passion, you must acquire and beget a temperance that may give it smoothness.   O, it offends me to the soul to hear a robustious[3] periwig-pated[4] fellow tear a passion to tat-

---

  1 " From fashion of himself," i.e., beside himself; out of his mind.

  2 " If she find him not," i.e., if she do not make him disclose his secret.

  3 Ranting; roaring.

  4 The periwig was a small wig worn by actors.   Periwigs were not worn

ters, to very rags, to split the ears of the groundlings,[1] who for the most part are capable of nothing but inexplicable dumb shows and noise. I would have such a fellow whipp'd for o'er-doing Termagant; it out-herods Herod :[2] pray you, avoid it.

First Player. I warrant your honor.

Hamlet. Be not too tame neither, but let your own discretion be your tutor: suit the action to the word, the word to the action, with this special observance, that you o'erstep not the modesty of nature; for anything so overdone is from the purpose of playing, whose end, both at the first and now, was and is, to hold, as 'twere, the mirror up to nature; to show virtue her own feature, scorn her own image, and the very age and body of the time his form and pressure.[3] Now, this overdone, or come tardy off, though it make the unskillful laugh, cannot but make the judicious grieve; the censure[4] of the which one must in your allowance[5] o'erweigh a whole theater of others. O, there be players that I have seen play, — and heard others praise, and that highly, — not to speak it profanely, that, neither having the accent of Christians, nor the gait of Christian, pagan, nor man, have so strutted and bellowed, that I have thought some of nature's journeymen had made men, and not made them well, they imitated humanity so abominably.

by gentlemen off the stage till the time of Charles II. Samuel Pepys notes in his Diary: " Nov. 8, 1663. — To church, where I found that my coming in a periwig did not prove so strange as I was afeard it would, for I thought all the church would presently have cast their eyes all upon me."

[1] Dr. Johnson notes that "the common people then [in Shakespeare's time] seem to have sat below, as they now sit in the upper gallery, who, not well understanding poetical language, were sometimes gratified by a mimical and mute representation ['dumb show'] of the drama previous to the dialogue."

[2] " Termagant " and " Herod " were personages who frequently appear in the Mysteries and Miracle Plays of the middle ages. They are always represented as violent characters, in which the ranting actor might show to advantage.

[3] " His form and pressure," i.e., its form and exact figure.

[4] Judgment.   [5] Opinion.

First Player. I hope we have reform'd that indifferently [1] with us, sir.

Hamlet. O, reform it altogether. And let those that play your clowns speak no more than is set down for them; [2] for there be of them that will themselves laugh, to set on some quantity of barren [3] spectators to laugh too; though, in the meantime, some necessary question of the play be then to be considered: that's villainous, and shows a most pitiful ambition in the fool that uses it. Go, make you ready.   [*Exeunt Players.*

Enter POLONIUS, ROSENCRANTZ, *and* GUILDENSTERN.

How now, my lord! will the King hear this piece of work?

Polonius. And the Queen too, and that presently.

Hamlet. Bid the players make haste. [*Exit Polonius.*] Will you two help to hasten them?

Rosencrantz. ⎱
Guildenstern. ⎰ We will, my lord.

                    [*Exeunt Rosencrantz and Guildenstern.*

Hamlet. What ho, Horatio!

Enter HORATIO.

Horatio. Here, sweet lord, at your service.

Hamlet. Horatio, thou art e'en as just a man
As e'er my conversation cop'd [4] withal.

---

1 Measurably.

2 Offhand buffoonery was very common with the stage clowns, many of them having great reputation for their improvised jokes. Johnson and Steevens (Shakespeare, edition 1785, p. 387) have this note: " Stowe informs us, that among the twelve players who were sworn the Queen's servants in 1583 were two rare men; viz., Thomas Wilson for a quick, delicate, refined *extemporall witte ;* and Richard Tarleton for a wondrous plentifull, pleasant *extemporall witt.*" Again, in Tarleton's News from Purgatory: " I absented myself from all plaies, as wanting that merrye Roscius of plaiers that famosed all comedies so with his pleasant and *extemporall invention.*"   3 Foolish.

4 " My conversation cop'd," i.e., encountered in my intercourse (with men).

Horatio. O, my dear lord,—

Hamlet. Nay, do not think I flatter;
For what advancement may I hope from thee
That no reven'ue hast but thy good spirits,
To feed and clothe thee ? Why should the poor be flatter'd ?
No, let the candied tongue lick ab'surd pomp,
And crook the pregnant [1] hinges of the knee
Where thrift may follow fawning. Dost thou hear ?
Since my dear soul was mistress of her choice,
And could of men distinguish, her election
Hath seal'd thee for herself; for thou hast been
As one, in suff'ring all, that suffers nothing;
A man that Fortune's buffets and rewards
Hast ta'en with equal thanks: and blest are those
Whose blood and judgment [2] are so well commingled
That they are not a pipe for Fortune's finger
To sound what stop [3] she please. Give me that man
That is not passion's slave, and I will wear him
In my heart's core, ay, in my heart of heart,
As I do thee.—Something too much of this.—
There is a play to-night before the King;
One scene of it comes near the circumstance,
Which I have told thee, of my father's death.
I prithee, when thou seest that act afoot,[4]
Even with the very comment of thy soul
Observe mine uncle: if his occulted [5] guilt
Do not itself unkennel in one speech,
It is a damned ghost that we have seen,
And my imaginations are as foul
As Vulcan's [6] stithy.[7] Give him heedful note;

[1] Ready.

[2] " Blood and judgment," i.e., passionate impulse and calm reason.

[3] The stops in a musical instrument are the holes on which the finger is placed to regulate the passage of the air, the sound.   [4] In progress.

[5] Concealed.   [6] See Note 5, p. 74.   [7] Smith's shop.

For I mine eyes will rivet to his face,
And after, we will both our judgments join
In censure of his seeming.[1]

   Horatio.   Well, my lord.
If he steal aught the whilst this play is playing,
And 'scape detecting, I will pay the theft.

   Hamlet. They are coming to the play; I must be idle:
Get you a place.

Danish march. A flourish. Enter KING, QUEEN, POLONIUS, OPHELIA,
ROSENCRANTZ, GUILDENSTERN, *and others.*

   King. How fares our cousin Hamlet?

   Hamlet. Excellent, i' faith; of the chameleon's dish:[2] I eat
the air, promise-cramm'd. You cannot feed capons so.

   King. I have nothing with this answer, Hamlet: these words
are not mine.

   Hamlet. No, nor mine now. [*To Polonius*] My lord, you play'd
once i' the university,[3] you say?

   Polonius. That did I, my lord; and was accounted a good
actor.

   Hamlet. What did you enact?

   Polonius. I did enact Julius Cæsar: I was killed i' the Capitol;[4] Brutus kill'd me.

---

[1] " Our judgments," etc., i.e., compare our opinions as to the impression
made on him.

[2] The body of the chameleon is so translucent, that the color of the animal
changes with the color of the objects near it. This apparently unsubstantial
nature of the chameleon doubtless gave rise to the popular belief that it fed
on air.

[3] " The practice of acting Latin plays [by undergraduates] in the univer-
sities of Oxford and Cambridge is very ancient, and continued to near the
middle of the last century. They were performed occasionally for the entertainment of princes and other great personages, and regularly at Christmas."
— MALONE.

[4] According to Plutarch, Cæsar was not assassinated in the Capitol, but in
the porch of Pompey's theater.

Hamlet. It was a brute part of him to kill so capital a calf there. — Be the players ready ?

Rosencrantz. Ay, my lord ; they stay upon your patience.

Queen. Come hither, my dear Hamlet, sit by me.

Hamlet. No, good mother, here's metal more attractive.

Polonius. [*To the King*] O, ho ! do you mark that ?

Hamlet. Lady, shall I lie in your lap ?

[*Lying down at Ophelia's feet.*

Ophelia. No, my lord.

Hamlet. I mean, my head upon your lap ?

Ophelia. You are merry, my lord.

Hamlet. Who, I ?

Ophelia. Ay, my lord.

Hamlet. O God, your only jig-maker.[1] What should a man do but be merry ? for, look you, how cheerfully my mother looks, and my father died within's [2] two hours.

Ophelia. Nay, 'tis twice two months, my lord.

Hamlet. So long ? Nay then, let the devil wear black, for I'll have a suit of sables.[3] O heavens ! die two months ago, and not forgotten yet ? Then there's hope a great man's memory may outlive his life half a year : but, by'r lady, he must build churches, then ; or else shall he suffer not thinking on, with the hobbyhorse,[4] whose epitaph is, " For, O, for, O, the hobbyhorse is forgot."

[1] A jig, in Shakespeare's day, was not only a dance, but also a ludicrous ballad or dialogue. In The Hog has lost his Pearl, published in 1614, one of the players comes in to solicit a gentleman to write a jig for him.

[2] Within this.

[3] " A suit of sables " was the richest and most magnificent dress that could be worn in Denmark.

[4] Furness (New Variorum Shakespeare, vol. iii. p. 249) quotes Nares' note describing the hobbyhorse : " A small horse ; also a personage belonging to the ancient morris dance when complete . . . being the figure of a horse fastened round the waist of a man, his own legs going through the body of the horse and enabling him to walk, but concealed by a long footcloth, while false legs appeared where those of the man should be, — at the sides of the horse."

Hautboys play.   The Dumb Show enters.

Enter a King *and a* Queen *very lovingly ; the* Queen *embracing him, and he her.   She kneels, and makes show of protestation unto him.   He takes her up, and declines his head upon her neck ; lays him down[1] upon a bank of flowers: she, seeing him asleep, leaves him.   Anon comes in a fellow, takes off his crown, kisses it, and pours poison in the* King's *ears, and exit.   The* Queen *returns, finds the* King *dead, and makes passionate action.   The* Poisoner, *with some two or three* Mutes, *comes in again, seeming to lament with her.   The dead body is carried away.   The* Poisoner *wooes the* Queen *with gifts: she seems loath and unwilling a while, but in the end accepts his love.*   [Exeunt.

Ophelia.   What means this, my lord ?

Hamlet.   Marry, this is miching mallecho;[2] it means mischief.

Ophelia.   Belike[3] this show imports the argument[4] of the play.

Enter Prologue.

Hamlet.   We shall know by this fellow : the players cannot keep counsel; they'll tell all.

Ophelia.   Will he tell us what this show meant ?

Hamlet.   Ay, or any show that you'll show him: be not you asham'd to show, he'll not shame to tell you what it means.

Ophelia.   You are naught, you are naught.   I'll mark the play.

Prologue.   For us, and for our tragedy,
                     Here stooping to your clemency,
                     We beg your hearing patiently.   [*Exit.*

Hamlet.   Is this a prologue, or the posy of a ring ?[5]

Ophelia.   'Tis brief, my lord.

Hamlet.   As woman's love.

---

1 " Lays him down," i.e., he lies down.

2 " Miching mallecho," i.e., secret mischief.

3 Probably.

4 Plot.

5 " Posy of a ring," i.e., the motto inscribed in a ring.   Such mottoes were often in verse, and necessarily brief.

Enter two Players, King, *and* Queen.

Player King. Full thirty times hath Phœbus'[1] cart[2] gone round
Neptune's salt wash,[3] and Tellus'[4] orbed ground,
And thirty dozen moons with borrow'd sheen[5]
About the world have times twelve thirties been,
Since love our hearts, and Hymen[6] did our hands,
Unite commutual in most sacred bands.

   Player Queen. So many journeys may the sun and moon
Make us again count o'er ere love be done!
But, woe is me, you are so sick of late,
So far from cheer and from your former state,
That I distrust you. Yet, though I distrust,
Discomfort you, my lord, it nothing must;
For women's fear and love holds quantity;
In neither aught, or in extremity.
Now, what my love is, proof hath made you know;
And as my love is siz'd, my fear is so.
Where love is great, the littlest doubts are fear;
Where little fears grow great, great love grows there.

   Player King. 'Faith, I must leave thee, love, and shortly too;
My operant[7] powers their functions leave[8] to do:
And thou shalt live in this fair world behind,
Honor'd, belov'd; and haply one as kind
For husband shalt thou—

   Player Queen.   O, confound the rest!
Such love must needs be treason in my breast:
In second husband let me be accurst!
None wed the second but who kill'd the first.

---

[1] Another name for Apollo, the god of day, and often used by the classic
poets to signify the sun.   [2] Car.
  [3] " Salt wash," i.e., the ocean; the briny sea.
  [4] The earth.
  [5] Luster.
  [6] The god of marriage.
  [7] Working; active.   [8] Cease.

Hamlet. [*Aside*] Wormwood, wormwood.

Player Queen. The instances [1] that second marriage move
Are base respects of thrift,[2] but none of love.

Player King. I do believe you think what now you speak;
But what we do determine oft we break.
Purpose is but the slave to memory,
Of violent birth, but poor validity;[3]
Which now, like fruit unripe, sticks on the tree,
But fall unshaken, when they mellow be.
Most necessary [4] 'tis that we forget
To pay ourselves what to ourselves is debt;
What to ourselves in passion we propose,
The passion ending, doth the purpose lose.
The violence of either grief or joy
Their own enactures [5] with themselves destroy:
Where joy most revels, grief doth most lament;
Grief joys, joy grieves, on slender accident.
This world is not for aye, nor 'tis not strange
That even our loves should with our fortunes change;
For 'tis a question left us yet to prove,
Whether love lead fortune, or else fortune love.
The great man down, you mark his favorite flies;
The poor advanc'd makes friends of enemies.
And hitherto doth love on fortune tend;[6]
For who not needs shall never lack a friend,
And who in want a hollow friend doth try,
Directly seasons [7] him his enemy.
But, orderly to end where I begun,
Our wills and fates do so contra'ry run,
That our devices still are overthrown;
Our thoughts are ours, their ends none of our own:

---

[1] Inducements.
[2] " Respects of thrift," i.e., considerations of gain.
[3] Value.   [4] Allowable.   [5] Resolutions.
[6] Attend.   [7] Ripens.

So think thou wilt no second husband wed;
But die thy thoughts when thy first lord is dead.

    Player Queen. Nor earth to me give food, nor heaven light!
Sport and repose lock from me day and night!
To desperation turn my trust and hope!
An anchor's cheer in prison be my scope![1]
Each opposite that blanks[2] the face of joy
Meet what I would have well, and it destroy!
Both here and hence pursue me lasting strife,
If, once a widow, ever I be wife!

    Hamlet. If she should break it now!

    Player King. 'Tis deeply sworn. Sweet, leave me here a while;
My spirits grow dull, and fain I would beguile
The tedious day with sleep.   [*Sleeps.*

    Player Queen.   Sleep rock thy brain;
And never come mischance between us twain!   [*Exit.*

    Hamlet. Madam, how like you this play?

    Queen. The lady doth protest too much, methinks.

    Hamlet. O, but she'll keep her word.

    King. Have you heard the argument? Is there no offense in't?

    Hamlet. No, no, they do but jest, poison in jest: no offense i' the world.

    King. What do you call the play?

    Hamlet. The Mouse-trap. Marry, how? Tropically.[3] This play is the image of a murder done in Vienna. Gonzago is the duke's name; his wife, Baptista. You shall see anon; 'tis a knavish piece of work; but what o' that? Your Majesty, and we that have free souls, it touches us not: let the gall'd jade wince,[4] our withers[5] are unwrung.

---

    [1] " An anchor's cheer," etc., i.e., may I be limited to an anchorite's (hermit's) fare and confinement.   [2] Blanches; makes pale.

    [3] Figuratively; from " trope," a rhetorical figure.

    [4] " Let the gall'd jade wince " was a proverbial saying.

    [5] The part of the horse, between the shoulders, on which the strain of the collar falls when the animal is pulling a load.

Enter LUCIANUS.

This is one Lucianus, nephew to the King.

Ophelia. You are as good as a chorus,[1] my lord.

Hamlet. I could interpret between you and your love, if I could see the puppets dallying.

Ophelia. Still better, and worse.

Hamlet. So you must take your husbands. — Begin, murderer; leave thy damnable faces, and begin. Come: "The croaking raven doth bellow for revenge."

Lucianus. Thoughts black, hands apt, drugs fit, and time
        agreeing;
   Confederate season,[2] else no creature seeing;
   Thou mixture rank, of midnight weeds collected,[3]
   With Hecate's [4] ban [5] thrice blasted, thrice infected,
   Thy natural magic and dire property
   On wholesome life usurp immediately.

                    [*Pours the poison into the sleeper's ears*

Hamlet. He poisons him i' the garden for's estate. His name's Gonzago: the story is extant, and writ in choice Italian. You shall see anon [6] how the murderer gets the love of Gonzago's wife.

Ophelia. The King rises.

Hamlet. What, frighted with false fire!

Queen. How fares my lord?

Polonius. Give o'er the play.

---

[1] The "chorus," in the sense in which Shakespeare uses it here, is a per sonage who explains the action of the play at its beginning, or at intervals of the performance; as in some of the poet's dramas, Henry V., for instance.

[2] "Confederate season," i.e., the time favoring.

[3] "Midnight weeds collected," since poisonous herbs were believed to be all the more noxious if gathered in the dark.

[4] A daughter of Perses and Asterias, known as Diana on the earth, Luna in heaven, and Hecate or Proserpina in the lower regions. She was supposed to preside over witchcraft and enchantments. In Shakespeare's verse the word always has two syllables, — Hec'ate.

[5] Curse.   [6] Soon.

King. Give me some light!—away!
All. Lights, lights, lights!

> [*Exeunt all but Hamlet and Horatio.*

Hamlet. Why, let the stricken deer go weep,
   The hart ungalled play;
  For some must watch, while some must sleep:
   So runs the world away.

Would not this, sir, and a forest of feathers,[1]—if the rest of my fortunes turn Turk with me,[2]—with two Provincial roses[3] on my raz'd shoes,[4] get me a fellowship in a cry[5] of players, sir?

Horatio. Half a share.[6]
Hamlet. A whole one, I.

  For thou dost know, O Damon dear!
   This realm dismantled was
  Of Jove himself; and now reigns here
   A very, very—pajock.[7]

Horatio. You might have rhym'd.
Hamlet. O good Horatio, I'll take the ghost's word for a thousand pound. Didst perceive?
Horatio. Very well, my lord.

---

[1] "A forest of feathers:" Malone notes that it appears from Dekker's Gull's Hornbook, that feathers were much worn on the stage in Shakespeare's time.

[2] "Turn Turk with me," i.e., deal cruelly with me. "To turn Turk and throw stones at the poor" was a proverbial expression for one who was tyrannical and hard-hearted.

[3] "Provincial roses," i.e., rosettes of ribbon in the form of roses of Provence.

[4] "Raz'd shoes," i.e., shoes slashed in the forepart with ornamental cuts.

[5] Company.

[6] Malone says, and refers to the Account of the Ancient Theaters, "The actors in our author's day did not have annual salaries, as at present. The whole receipts of the theater were divided into shares, . . . and each actor had one or more shares or part of share, according to his merit."

[7] Peacock.

Hamlet. Upon the talk of poisoning?

Horatio. I did very well note him.

Hamlet. Ah, ha! Come, some music! come, the recorders![1]

> For if the King like not the comedy,
> Why, then, belike, he likes it not, perdy.[2]

Come, some music!

Reënter ROSENCRANTZ *and* GUILDENSTERN.

Guildenstern. Good my lord, vouchsafe me a word with you.

Hamlet. Sir, a whole history.

Guildenstern. The King, sir,—

Hamlet. Ay, sir, what of him?

Guildenstern. Is in his retirement marvelous distemper'd.[3]

Hamlet. With drink, sir?

Guildenstern. No, my lord, rather with choler.

Hamlet. Your wisdom should show itself more richer[4] to signify this to his doctor; for, for me to put him to his purgation would perhaps plunge him into far more choler.

Guildenstern. Good my lord, put your discourse into some frame,[5] and start not so wildly from my affair.

Hamlet. I am tame, sir: pronounce.

Guildenstern. The Queen your mother, in most great affliction of spirit, hath sent me to you.

Hamlet. You are welcome.

Guildenstern. Nay, good my lord, this courtesy is not of the right breed. If it shall please you to make me a wholesome answer, I will do your mother's commandment: if not, your pardon and my return shall be the end of my business.

Hamlet. Sir, I cannot.

Guildenstern. What, my lord?

[1] A musical instrument resembling a flageolet.

[2] Corrupted from the French *par Dieu.*

[3] Disordered.   [4] See Note 5, p. 53.

[5] Coherence.

Hamlet. Make you a wholesome answer; my wit's diseased: but, sir, such answer as I can make, you shall command; or, rather, as you say, my mother: therefore no more, but to the matter. My mother, you say,—

Rosencrantz. Then, thus she says: your behavior hath struck her into amazement and admiration.[1]

Hamlet. O wonderful son, that can so astonish a mother! But is there no sequel at the heels of this mother's admiration? Impart.

Rosencrantz. She desires to speak with you in her closet ere you go to bed.

Hamlet. We shall obey, were she ten times our mother. Have you any further trade with us?

Rosencrantz. My lord, you once did love me.

Hamlet. So I do still, by these pickers and stealers.[2]

Rosencrantz. Good my lord, what is your cause of distemper? you do, surely, bar the door upon your own liberty, if you deny your griefs to your friend.

Hamlet. Sir, I lack advancement.

Rosencrantz. How can that be, when you have the voice of the King himself for your succession in Denmark?

Hamlet. Ay, sir, but "While the grass grows,"—the proverb is something musty.

Reënter Players *with recorders.*

O, the recorders! let me see one.—To withdraw with you:— why do you go about to recover the wind of me,[3] as if you would drive me into a toil?

[1] Wonder.

[2] "'Hands,' says Dr. Johnson, and rightly. But the phrase is taken from our [English] Church Catechism, where the catechumen, in his duty to his neighbor, is taught to keep his hands from 'picking and stealing.'" —WHALLEY.

[3] "Recover the wind of me" is a hunting phrase, and means to cause the game to run with the wind, that it may not scent the snare toward which it is driven.

Guildenstern. O, my lord, if my duty be too bold, my love is too unmannerly.

Hamlet. I do not well understand that. Will you play upon this pipe ?

Guildenstern. My lord, I cannot.

Hamlet. I pray you.

Guildenstern. Believe me, I cannot.

Hamlet. I do beseech you.

Guildenstern. I know no touch of it, my lord.

Hamlet. 'Tis as easy as lying : govern these ventages [1] with your fingers and thumb, give it breath with your mouth, and it will discourse most eloquent music. Look you, these are the stops.

Guildenstern. But these cannot I command to any utterance of harmony : I have not the skill.

Hamlet. Why, look you now, how unworthy a thing you make of me ! You would play upon me ; you would seem to know my stops ; you would pluck out the heart of my mystery ; you would sound me from my lowest note to the top of my compass : [2] and there is much music, excellent voice, in this little organ ; yet cannot you make it speak. 'Sblood, do you think I am easier to be play'd on than a pipe ? Call me what instrument you will, though you can fret [3] me, yet you cannot play upon me.—

Enter POLONIUS.

God bless you, sir !

Polonius. My lord, the Queen would speak with you, and presently. [4]

Hamlet. Do you see yonder cloud that's almost in shape of a camel ?

Polonius. By the mass, and 'tis like a camel, indeed.

---

[1] Holes.

[2] " The range of a musical instrument, from its highest to its lowest note."

[3] Annoy ; with a play on the word " fret," in its meaning of " stop," or guide to the fingers on the strings of a guitar.   [4] Immediately.

Hamlet. Methinks it is like a weasel.

Polonius. It is back'd like a weasel.

Hamlet. Or like a whale?

Polonius. Very like a whale.

Hamlet. Then I will come to my mother by and by. [*Aside*] They fool me to the top of my bent.[1]—I will come by and by.

Polonius. I will say so.

Hamlet. By and by is easily said. [*Exit Polonius.*] Leave me, friends.   [*Exeunt all but Hamlet.*

'Tis now the very witching time of night,

When churchyards yawn, and hell itself breathes out

Contagion to this world: now could I drink hot blood,

And do such bitter business as the day

Would quake to look on. Soft! now to my mother.

O heart, lose not thy nature; let not ever

The soul of Nero[2] enter this firm bosom:

Let me be cruel, not unnatural.

I will speak daggers to her, but use none;

My tongue and soul in this be hypocrites:

How in my words soever she be shent,[3]

To give them seals[4] never, my soul, consent!   [*Exit.*

SCENE III. *A Room in the Castle.*

Enter KING, ROSENCRANTZ, *and* GUILDENSTERN.

King. I like him not, nor stands it safe with us

To let his madness range. Therefore prepare you:

I your commission will forthwith dispatch,

And he to England shall along with you.

---

1 " Top of my bent," i.e., utmost.

2 Lucius Domitius Nero was one of the most dissolute and cruel of the Roman emperors. He caused his mother's assassination, and murdered his divorced wife; and " popular suspicion pointed to him as the author of the conflagration " when Rome was burned A. D. 64.

3 Reproached.   4 Deeds.

The terms of our estate may not endure
Hazard so near us as doth hourly grow
Out of his lunacies.

    Guildenstern.   We will ourselves provide.
Most holy and religious fear it is
To keep those many many bodies safe
That live and feed upon your Majesty.

    Rosencrantz. The single and peculiar life [1] is bound,
With all the strength and armor of the mind,
To keep itself from noyance; [2] but much more
That spirit upon whose weal [3] depend and rest
The lives of many.   The cease [4] of majesty
Dies not alone, but like a gulf doth draw
What's near it with it: it is a massy wheel,
Fix'd on the summit of the highest mount,
To whose huge spokes ten thousand lesser things
Are mortis'd and adjoin'd; which, when it falls,
Each small annexment, petty consequence,
Attends the boisterous ruin.   Never alone
Did the King sigh, but with a general groan.

    King. Arm you, I pray you, to this speedy voyage;
For we will fetters put upon this fear, [5]
Which now goes too free-footed.

    Guildenstern. ⎱
    Rosencrantz. ⎰   We will haste us.

                [Exeunt Rosencrantz and Guildenstern.

Enter POLONIUS.

    Polonius. My lord, he's going to his mother's closet.
Behind the arras I'll convey myself,
To hear the process; I'll warrant she'll tax him home: [6]
And as you said, and wisely was it said,

---

  1 "The single and peculiar life," i.e., the private individual.
  2 Harm.   3 Welfare.   4 Decease.   5 The object of fear.
  6 "Tax him home," i.e., rate him soundly.

'Tis meet that some more audience than a mother,
Since nature makes them partial, should o'erhear
The speech, of vantage.[1]   Fare you well, my liege:
I'll call upon you ere you go to bed,
And tell you what I know.

    King.   Thanks, dear my lord.

                                  [Exit Polonius.

O, my offense is rank, it smells to heaven;
It hath the primal eldest curse upon't,
A brother's murder.   Pray can I not,
Though inclination be as sharp as will:
My stronger guilt defeats my strong intent;
And, like a man to double business bound,
I stand in pause where I shall first begin,
And both neglect.   What if this cursed hand
Were thicker than itself with brother's blood,
Is there not rain enough in the sweet heavens
To wash it white as snow?   Whereto serves mercy
But to confront[2] the visage of offense?
And what's in prayer but this twofold force,—
To be forestalled ere we come to fall,
Or pardon'd being down?[3]   Then I'll look up:
My fault is past.   But, O, what form of prayer
Can serve my turn?   "Forgive me my foul murder?"
That cannot be; since I am still possess'd
Of those effects for which I did the murder,—
My crown, mine own ambition, and my Queen.
May one be pardon'd, and retain the offense?
In the corrupted currents of this world
Offense's gilded hand[4] may shove by justice,

---

   [1] " Of vantage," i.e., " from the vantage ground of concealment."

   [2] Face, or face down.

   [3] " Forestalled," etc., i.e., to be delivered from the temptation of sin, or pardoned after its commission.

   [4] " Offense's gilded hand," i.e., the offender's gold.

And oft 'tis seen the wicked prize itself
Buys out the law; but 'tis not so above:
There is no shuffling, there the action lies [1]
In his [2] true nature; and we ourselves compell'd,
Even to the teeth and forehead of our faults,
To give in evidence.   What then? what rests? [3]
Try what repentance can: what can it not?
Yet what can it when one can not repent?
·O wretched state! O bosom black as death!
O limed [4] soul, that, struggling to be free,
Art more engag'd!   Help, angels!   Make assay!
Bow, stubborn knees; and, heart with strings of steel,
Be soft as sinews of the new-born babe!
All may be well.   *[Retires and kneels.*

Enter HAMLET.

Hamlet.   Now might I do it pat, [5] now he is praying;
And now I'll do it.   And so he goes to heaven;
And so am I reveng'd.   That would be scann'd:
A villain kills my father; and for that,
I, his sole son, do this same villain send
To heaven.
O, this is hire and salary, not revenge.
He took my father grossly, full of bread; [6]
With all his crimes broad blown, as flush as May;
And how his audit [7] stands who knows save Heaven?
But in our circumstance and course of thought,
'Tis heavy with him; and am I then reveng'd,

---

[1] Is to be maintained; the legal sense of the word.

[2] See Note 1, p. 39.   [3] Remains.

[4] As with birdlime, a viscous substance with which fowlers smeared the twigs and branches near birds' nests.   The feet of the birds becoming entangled in it, the hunter easily captured his prey.

[5] This moment.

[6] " Full of bread," i.e., in luxurious living.

[7] Account.

To take him in the purging of his soul,
When he is fit and season'd for his passage?
No!
Up, sword, and know thou a more horrid hent.[1]
When he is drunk, asleep, or in his rage,
At gaming, swearing, or about some act
That has no relish of salvation in't,
Then trip him, that his heels may kick at heaven,
And that his soul may be as damn'd and black
As hell, whereto it goes.   My mother stays:
This physic but prolongs thy sickly days.   [*Exit.*

   King. [*Rising*] My words fly up, my thoughts remain below:
Words without thoughts never to heaven go.   [*Exit.*

SCENE IV.   *The Queen's Closet.*

Enter QUEEN *and* POLONIUS.

   Polonius. He will come straight.[2] Look you lay home to him:
Tell him his pranks have been too broad to bear with,
And that your Grace hath screen'd and stood between
Much heat and him.   I'll sconce [3] me even here.
Pray you, be round with him.

   Hamlet. [*Within*] Mother, mother, mother!

   Queen.   I'll warrant you,
Fear me not.   Withdraw, I hear him coming.

           [*Polonius hides behind the arras.*

Enter HAMLET.

   Hamlet. Now, mother, what's the matter?
   Queen. Hamlet, thou hast thy father much offended.
   Hamlet. Mother, you have my father much offended.

---

[1] Hold, or purpose.
[2] Straightway; without delay.   [3] Hide.

Queen. Come, come, you answer with an idle tongue.

Hamlet. Go, go, you question with a wicked tongue.

Queen. Why, how now, Hamlet !

Hamlet.   What's the matter now ?

Queen. Have you forgot me ?

Hamlet.   No, by the rood,[1] not so

You are the Queen, your husband's brother's wife ;

And—would it were not so !—you are my mother.

Queen. Nay, then, I'll set those to you that can speak.

Hamlet. Come, come, and sit you down ; you shall not budge :

You go not till I set you up a glass

Where you may see the inmost part of you.

Queen. What wilt thou do ? thou wilt not murder me ?

Help, help, ho !

Polonius. [*Behind*] What, ho ! help, help, help !

Hamlet. [*Drawing*] How now ! a rat ?   Dead, for a ducat,
          dead !   [*Makes a pass through the arras.*

Polonius. [*Behind*] O, I am slain !   [*Falls and dies.*

Queen. O me, what hast thou done ?

Hamlet.   Nay, I know not:

Is it the King ?

Queen. O, what a rash and bloody deed is this !

Hamlet. A bloody deed ! almost as bad, good mother,

As kill a king, and marry with his brother.

Queen. As kill a king !

Hamlet.   Ay, lady, 'twas my word.—

                    [*Lifts up the arras, and discovers Polonius.*

Thou wretched, rash, intruding fool, farewell !

I took thee for thy better : take thy fortune ;

Thou find'st to be too busy is some danger.—

Leave wringing of your hands.   Peace ! sit you down,

And let me wring your heart ; for so I shall,

If it be made of penetrable stuff,

1 Crucifix. " It would appear that in earlier times the rood signified not merely the cross, but the image of Christ upon it."—DYCE.

If damned custom have not brass'd it so
That it be proof and bulwark against sense.[1]

Queen. What have I done, that thou dar'st wag thy tongue
In noise so rude against me ?

Hamlet.   Such an act
That blurs the grace and blush of modesty ;
Calls virtue hypocrite ; takes off the rose
From the fair forehead of an innocent love,
And sets a blister there ; makes marriage vows
As false as dicers' oaths : O, such a deed
As from the body of contraction[2] plucks
The very soul, and sweet religion makes
A rhapsody of words : heaven's face doth glow ;
Yea, this solidity and compound mass,[3]
With tristful visage, as against the doom,
Is thought-sick at the act.

Queen.   Ah me, what act,
That roars so loud, and thunders in the index ?[4]

Hamlet. Look here, upon this picture, and on this,
The counterfeit presentment[5] of two brothers.
See, what a grace was seated on this brow ;
Hyperion's[6] curls ; the front[7] of Jove[8] himself ;
An eye like Mars,[9] to threaten and command ;

---

[1] Feeling.   [2] The marriage contract.

[3] " Solidity and compound mass," i.e., the solid earth.

[4] Shakespeare uses " index " for title or prologue. " The index was formerly placed at the beginning of a book, not at the end, as now." — EDWARDS.

[5] " Counterfeit presentment," i.e., portrait or likeness.

[6] See Note 6, p. 31.

[7] The face and head.

[8] " Jupiter, Jove, or Zeus, king of the gods, supreme ruler of the universe, . . . the most prominent of all the Olympian divinities : the others were obliged to submit to his will, and trembled at his all-powerful nod." — GUERBER : *Myths of Greece and Rome*, p. 39.

[9] See Note 6, p. 74.

A station[1] like the herald Mercury[2]
New-lighted on a heaven-kissing hill;
A combination and a form indeed,
Where every god did seem to set his seal,
To give the world assurance of a man:
This was your husband.   Look you now what follows.
Here is your husband; like a mildew'd ear,
Blasting his wholesome brother.[3]   Have you eyes?
Could you on this fair mountain leave to feed,
And batten[4] on this moor?   Ha! have you eyes?
You cannot call it love; for at your age
The heyday in the blood is tame, it's humble,
And waits upon the judgment; and what judgment
Would step from this to this?   Sense, sure, you have,
Else could you not have motion; but sure, that sense
Is apoplex'd; for madness would not err,
Nor sense to ecstasy was ne'er so thrall'd[5]
But it reserv'd some quantity of choice,
To serve in such a difference.   What devil was't
That thus hath cozen'd you at hoodman blind?[6]
Eyes without feeling, feeling without sight,
Ears without hands or eyes, smelling sans[7] all,
Or but a sickly part of one true sense
Could not so mope.[8]

    Queen.   O Hamlet, speak no more!
Thou turn'st mine eyes into my very soul;
And there I see such black and grained spots

---

1 Attitude; presence.
2 "Mercury," son of Jupiter and Maia, messenger of the gods, and patron of travelers, merchants, etc., was remarkable for his agility and graceful movement.
3 See Gen. xli. 5–7.
4 Feed grossly.   5 Enslaved.
6 "Hoodman blind," i.e., blindman's buff.
7 A French word signifying "without."
8 "So mope," i.e., be so dull.

As will not leave their tinct.[1]
These words, like daggers, enter in mine ears:
No more, sweet Hamlet!

 Hamlet.   A murderer and a villain;
A slave that is not twentieth part the tithe
Of your precedent lord; a vice of kings;[2]
A cutpurse of the empire and the rule,
That from a shelf the precious diadem stole,
And put it in his pocket!

 Queen.   No more!
 Hamlet. A king of shreds and patches,—

Enter GHOST.

Save me, and hover o'er me with your wings,
You heavenly guards!—What would your gracious figure?

 Queen. Alas, he's mad!
 Hamlet. Do you not come your tardy son to chide,
That, laps'd in time and passion,[3] lets go by
The important acting of your dread command?
O, say!

 Ghost. Do not forget. This visitation
Is but to whet thy almost blunted purpose.
But, look, amazement on thy mother sits:
O, step between her and her fighting soul;
Conceit[4] in weakest bodies strongest works.
Speak to her, Hamlet.

 Hamlet.   How is it with you, lady?

---

[1] "Such black and grained spots," etc., i.e., stains so thoroughly ingrained that they cannot be removed.

[2] "A vice of kings," i.e., a buffoon king; alluding to the vice, or clown, in the old Moral Plays, in which vice and virtue were frequently personated.

[3] "Laps'd in time and passion" is thus explained by Dr. Johnson: "that having suffered time to slip, and passion to cool, lets go by," etc.

[4] Imagination.

Queen. Alas, how is't with you,
That you do bend your eye on vacancy,
And with the incorporal [1] air do hold discourse ?
Forth at your eyes your spirits wildly peep ;
And, as the sleeping soldiers in the alarm,
Your bedded hair, like life in excrements,[2]
Starts up, and stands on end.   O gentle son,
Upon the heat and flame of thy distemper
Sprinkle cool patience.   Whereon do you look ?
Hamlet. On him, on him !   Look you, how pale he glares !
His form and cause conjoin'd, preaching to stones,
Would make them capable.[3] — Do not look upon me ;
Lest with this piteous action you convert
My stern effects :[4] then what I have to do
Will want true color ; tears, perchance, for blood.
Queen. To whom do you speak this ?
Hamlet.   Do you see nothing there ?
Queen. Nothing at all ; yet all that is I see.
Hamlet. Nor did you nothing hear ?
Queen.   No, nothing but ourselves.
Hamlet. Why, look you there ! look, how it steals away !
My father, in his habit as he liv'd !
Look, where he goes, even now, out at the portal !

[*Exit Ghost.*

Queen. This is the very coinage of your brain :
This bodiless creation ecstasy
Is very cunning in.
Hamlet.   Ecstasy !
My pulse, as yours, doth temperately keep time,
And makes as healthful music.   It is not madness
That I have utter'd : bring me to the test,

Ghost appears
to give
Hamlet
courage

---

[1] Bodiless.
[2] " Life in excrements," i.e., in such excrescences as hair, nails, etc.,
which have no life in themselves.
[3] Susceptible.   [4] Purposes or resolutions.

And I the matter will reword, which madness
Would gambol from.   Mother, for love of grace,
Lay not that flattering unction to your soul,
That not your trespass, but my madness, speaks:
It will but skin and film the ulcerous place,
Whiles rank corruption, mining all within,
Infects unseen.   Confess yourself to Heaven;
Repent what's past; avoid what is to come;
And do not spread the compost on the weeds,
To make them ranker.   Forgive me this my virtue;
For in the fatness of these pursy times [1]
Virtue itself of vice must pardon beg,
Yea, curb and woo for leave to do him good.

   Queen. O Hamlet, thou hast cleft my heart in twain.

   Hamlet. O, throw away the worser part of it,
And live the purer with the other half.
Good night; but go not to mine uncle's bed:
Assume a virtue, if you have it not.
That monster, custom, who all sense doth eat,
Of habits devil, is angel yet in this,
That to the use of actions fair and good
He likewise gives a frock or livery,
That aptly is put on. [2]
For use almost can change the stamp of nature,
And either master the devil, or throw him out
With wondrous potency.   Once more, good night;
And when you are desirous to be bless'd,
I'll blessing beg of you.   For this same lord,

                                          [Pointing to Polonius.

---

[1] " Fatness of these pursy times," i.e., times grown insolent through
gross indulgence.

[2] "That monster, custom," etc., i. e. (to paraphrase the passage), that
monster, custom, which by " mere repetition " destroys in us the sense of evil
in our bad actions, is an angel in this, that by the same habitual use it makes
easy the practice of that which is good.

I do repent; but Heaven hath pleas'd it so,
To punish me with this, and this with me,
That I must be their scourge and minister.
I will bestow [1] him, and will answer well
The death I gave him.   So, again, good night.
I must be cruel, only to be kind:
Thus bad begins, and worse remains behind.
One word more, good lady.

    Queen.   What shall I do?

    Hamlet. Not this, by no means, that I bid you do:
Let the bloat King pinch wanton on your cheek;
Make you to ravel all this matter out,
That I essentially am not in madness,
But mad in craft.   'Twere good you let him know;
For who, that's but a queen, fair, sober, wise,
Would from a paddock,[2] from a bat, a gib,[3]
Such dear concernings hide? who would do so?
No, in despite of sense and secrecy,
Unpeg the basket on the house's top,
Let the birds fly, and, like the famous ape,
To try conclusions,[4] in the basket creep,
And break your own neck down.

    Queen. Be thou assur'd, if words be made of breath,
And breath of life, I have no life to breathe
What thou hast said to me.

    Hamlet. I must to England; you know that?

    Queen.   Alack,
I had forgot: 'tis so concluded on.

    Hamlet. There's letters seal'd; and my two schoolfellows,
Whom I will trust as I will adders fang'd,[5]
They bear the mandate; they must sweep my way,
And marshal me to knavery.   Let it work;

---

[1] Find a place for.   [2] A toad.   [3] A cat.
[4] Experiments.
[5] Still having their fangs.

For 'tis the sport to have the enginer [1]
Hoist [2] with his own petar: [3] and't shall go hard
But I will delve one yard below their mines,
And blow them at the moon.   O, 'tis most sweet,
When in one line two crafts directly meet !
This man shall set me packing:
I'll lug the corse into the neighbor [4] room.
Mother, good night.   Indeed this counselor
Is now most still, most secret, and most grave,
Who was in life a foolish, prating knave. —
Come, sir, to draw toward an end with you. —
Good night, mother.

> [*Exeunt severally; Hamlet dragging in Polonius.*

ACT IV.

Scene I.   *A Room in the Castle.*

Enter King, Queen, Rosencrantz, *and* Guildenstern.

King.   There's matter in these sighs: these profound heaves
You must translate; 'tis fit we understand them.
Where is your son ?

Queen.   Bestow this place on us a little while.

> [*Exeunt Rosencrantz and Guildenstern.*

Ah, mine own lord, what have I seen to-night !

King.   What, Gertrude ?   How does Hamlet ?

Queen.   Mad as the sea and wind when both contend
Which is the mightier.   In his lawless fit,
Behind the arras hearing something stir,
Whips out his rapier, cries, " A rat, a rat ! "
And in this brainish [5] apprehension kills
The unseen good old man.

---

[1] Engineer.   [2] Hoisted; blown up.   [3] Petard.
[4] Neighboring.   [5] Crazy.

King.   O heavy deed !
It had been so with us, had we been there.
His liberty is full of threats to all ;
To you yourself, to us,[1] to everyone.
Alas ! how shall this bloody deed be answer'd ?
It will be laid to us, whose providence [2]
Should have kept short, restrain'd, and out of haunt,[3]
This mad young man : but so much was our love,
We would not understand what was most fit ;
But like the owner of a foul disease,
To keep it from divulging, let it feed
Even on the pith of life.   Where is he gone ?
    Queen. To draw apart [4] the body he hath kill'd ;
O'er whom his very madness, like some ore [5]
Among a mineral [6] of metals base,
Shows itself pure.   He weeps for what is done.
    King. O Gertrude, come away !
The sun no sooner shall the mountains touch
But we will ship him hence ; and this vile deed
We must, with all our majesty and skill,
Both countenance and excuse. — Ho, Guildenstern !

Reënter ROSENCRANTZ *and* GUILDENSTERN.

Friends both, go join you with some further aid.
Hamlet in madness hath Polonius slain,
And from his mother's closet hath he dragg'd him.
Go seek him out ; speak fair,[7] and bring the body
Into the chapel.   I pray you, haste in this.
                    [*Exeunt Rosencrantz and Guildenstern*
Come, Gertrude, we'll call up our wisest friends,

---

1 " To us," i.e., to myself ; the King using the royal style.
2 Precaution.
3 " Out of haunt," i.e., in seclusion ; away from company.
4 Aside.   5 Precious ore ; gold.   6 Mine.
7 Gently.

And let them know both what we mean to do,
And what's untimely done: so, haply, slander,
Whose whisper o'er the world's diameter,
As level as the cannon to his blank,[1]
Transports his poison'd shot, may miss our name,
And hit the woundless air.   O, come away!
My soul is full of discord and dismay.   [*Exeunt.*

Scene II. *Another Room in the Castle.*

Enter HAMLET.

Hamlet. Safely stowed.

Rosencrantz. ⎫
Guildenstern. ⎭ [*Within*] Hamlet! Lord Hamlet!

Hamlet. But soft, what noise? who calls on Hamlet?   O,
here they come.

Enter ROSENCRANTZ *and* GUILDENSTERN.

Rosencrantz. What have you done, my lord, with the dead
body?

Hamlet. Compounded it with dust, whereto 'tis kin.

Rosencrantz. Tell us where 'tis, that we may take it thence,
And bear it to the chapel.

Hamlet. Do not believe it.

Rosencrantz. Believe what?

Hamlet. That I can keep your counsel, and not mine own.
Besides, to be demanded of a sponge, what replication[2] should
be made by the son of a king?

Rosencrantz. Take you me for a sponge, my lord?

Hamlet. Ay, sir, that soaks up the King's countenance,[3] his rewards, his authorities.   But such officers do the King best service

---

1 The white spot in the center of the target; from the French *blanc*
("white").

2 Reply; a legal term in the course of pleading.

3 Favor.

in the end: he keeps them, like an ape doth nuts, in the corner
of his jaw;[1] first mouth'd, to be last swallowed: when he needs
what you have glean'd, it is but squeezing you, and, sponge, you
shall be dry again.

Rosencrantz. I understand you not, my lord.

Hamlet. I am glad of it: a knavish speech sleeps in a foolish ear.

Rosencrantz. My lord, you must tell us where the body is, and
go with us to the King.

Hamlet. The body is with the King, but the King is not with
the body. The King is a thing —

Guildenstern. A thing, my lord !

Hamlet. Of nothing: bring me to him. Hide, fox, and all
after.[2]　　　　　　　　　　　　　　　　　　　　　　　　　[*Exeunt.*

SCENE III. *Another Room in the Castle.*

Enter KING, *attended.*

King. I have sent to seek him, and to find the body.
How dangerous is it that this man goes loose !
Yet must not we put the strong law on him:
He's lov'd of the distracted multitude,
Who like not in their judgment, but their eyes;
And where 'tis so, the offender's scourge[3] is weigh'd,
But never the offense. To bear all smooth and even,
This sudden sending him away must seem
Deliberate pause: diseases desperate grown,
By desperate appliance are reliev'd,
Or not at all.—

Enter ROSENCRANTZ.

How now ! what hath befall'n ?

---

[1] "Ape doth nuts," etc. "It is the way of monkeys in eating to throw
that part of their food which they take up first into a pouch they are provided
with on the side of the jaw, and there they keep it till they have done with
the rest." — JOHNSON.

[2] The children's game of "whoop," or "hide and seek."

[3] Punishment.

Rosencrantz. Where the dead body is bestow'd, my lord,
We cannot get from him.

King.   But where is he?

Rosencrantz. Without, my lord; guarded, to know your pleasure.

King. Bring him before us.

Rosencrantz. Ho, Guildenstern! bring in my lord.

Enter HAMLET *and* GUILDENSTERN.

King. Now, Hamlet, where's Polonius?

Hamlet. At supper.

King. At supper! where?

Hamlet. Not where he eats, but where he is eaten: a certain convocation of politic worms are e'en at him. Your worm is your only emperor for diet: we fat all creatures else to fat us, and we fat ourselves for maggots. Your fat king and your lean beggar is but variable[1] service,—two dishes, but to one table: that's the end.

King. Alas, alas!

Hamlet. A man may fish with the worm that hath eat of a king, and eat of the fish that hath fed of that worm.

King. What dost thou mean by this?

Hamlet. Nothing but to show you how a king may go a progress[2] through the body of a beggar.

King. Where is Polonius?

Hamlet. In heaven; send thither to see: if your messenger find him not there, seek him i' the other place yourself. But indeed, if you find him not within this month, you shall nose him as you go up the stairs into the lobby.

King. Go seek him there.   [*To some Attendants.*

Hamlet. He will stay till you come.   [*Exeunt Attendants.*

King. Hamlet, this deed, for thine especial safety,—
Which we do tender,[3] as we dearly grieve

[1] Varied.
[2] The journeys of state through the country by the kings of England were called "progresses."
[3] "Do tender," i.e., have at heart.

For that which thou hast done,— must send thee hence
With fiery quickness: therefore prepare thyself.
The bark is ready, and the wind at help,[1]
The associates tend,[2] and everything is bent
For England.

    Hamlet.   For England !

    King.   Ay, Hamlet.

    Hamlet.   Good.

    King. So is it, if thou knew'st our purposes.

    Hamlet. I see a cherub that sees them. But, come; for England ! Farewell, dear mother.

    King. Thy loving father, Hamlet.

    Hamlet. My mother: father and mother is man and wife; man and wife is one flesh; and so, my mother.   Come, for England !
                                          [Exit.

    King. Follow him at foot;[3] tempt him with speed aboard;
Delay it not; I'll have him hence to-night.
Away ! for everything is seal'd and done
That else leans on the affair: pray you, make haste.

                  [Exeunt Rosencrantz and Guildenstern.

And, England, if my love thou hold'st at aught,[4]—
As my great power thereof may give thee sense,
Since yet thy cicatrice[5] looks raw and red
After the Danish sword, and thy free awe[6]
Pays homage to us,—thou mayst not coldly set[7]
Our sovereign process, which imports at full,
By letters con'juring to that effect,
The present death of Hamlet.   Do it, England;

    1 " At help," i.e., favorable.

    2 " Associates tend," i.e., companions wait.

    3 " Follow him at foot," i.e., follow close on his footsteps.

    4 " Thou hold'st at aught," i.e., has any value with you.

    5 Scar.

    6 " Free awe," i.e., awe still felt, though Danish arms are no longer enforcing it.

    7 " Coldly set," i.e., treat coldly, or with indifference.

For like the hectic [1] in my blood he rages,
And thou must cure me.   Till I know 'tis done,
Howe'er my haps,[2] my joys were ne'er begun.   [*Exit.*

Scene IV.   *A Plain in Denmark.*

Enter Fortinbras, *a* Captain, *and* Soldiers, *marching.*

Fortinbras. Go, captain, from me greet the Danish King;
Tell him that, by his license, Fortinbras
Craves the conveyance of a promis'd march
Over his kingdom.   You know the rendezvous.
If that his Majesty would aught with us,
We shall express our duty in his eye ; [3]
And let him know so.
    Captain.   I will do't, my lord.
    Fortinbras. Go softly [4] on.   [*Exeunt Fortinbras and Soldiers.*

Enter Hamlet, Rosencrantz, Guildenstern, *and others.*

Hamlet. Good sir, whose powers are these ? [5]
Captain. They are of Norway, sir.
Hamlet. How purpos'd, sir, I pray you ?
Captain. Against some part of Poland.
Hamlet. Who commands them, sir ?
Captain. The nephew to old Norway, Fortinbras.
Hamlet. Goes it against the main of Poland, sir,
Or for some frontier ?
    Captain. Truly to speak, and with no addition,
We go to gain a little patch of ground
That hath in it no profit but the name.
To pay five ducats, five, I would not farm [6] it ;

[1] Fever.
[2] "Howe'er my haps," i.e., whatever happens to me.
[3] "In his eye," i.e., in his presence.   [4] Gently.
[5] "Whose powers are these ? " i.e., whose army is this?
[6] Rent.

Nor will it yield to Norway [1] or the Pole
A ranker [2] rate, should it be sold in fee. [3]
   Hamlet. Why, then the Polack [4] never will defend it.
   Captain. Yes, it is already garrison'd.
   Hamlet. Two thousand souls and twenty thousand ducats
Will not debate [5] the question of this straw:
This is the imposthume of much wealth and peace,
That inward breaks, and shows no cause without
Why the man dies.   I humbly thank you, sir.
   Captain. God be wi' you, [6] sir.   [*Exit.*
   Rosencrantz.   Will't please you go, my lord?
   Hamlet. I'll be with you straight.   Go a little before.
                   [*Exeunt all except Hamlet.*

How all occasions do inform against me,
And spur my dull revenge!   What is a man,
If his chief good and market [7] of his time
Be but to sleep and feed? a beast, no more.
Sure, He that made us with such large discourse, [8]
Looking before and after, gave us not
That capability and godlike reason
To fust [9] in us unus'd.   Now, whether it be
Bestial oblivion, or some craven scruple
Of thinking too precisely on the event,—
A thought which, quarter'd, hath but one part wisdom
And ever three parts coward,— I do not know
Why yet I live to say, "This thing's to do,"
Sith I have cause and will and strength and means
To do't.   Examples gross as earth exhort me:

1 The King of Norway.   2 Higher.
3 " In fee," i.e., outright; in fee simple.
4 " The Polack," i.e., the Polanders collectively.
5 Fight over.
6 See Note 2, p. 76.
7 Trade; business; occupation.
8 " Large discourse," i.e., range of comprehension.
9 Grow stale.

Witness this army, of such mass and charge,
Led by a delicate and tender prince,
Whose spirit, with divine ambition puff'd,[1]
Makes mouths at the invisible event,
Exposing what is mortal and unsure
To all that fortune, death, and danger dare,
Even for an eggshell.   Rightly to be great
Is not to stir without great argument,[2]
But greatly to find quarrel in a straw,
When honor's at the stake.   How stand I, then,
That have a father kill'd, a mother stain'd,
Excitements of my reason and my blood,[3]
And let all sleep ? while, to my shame, I see
The imminent death of twenty thousand men,
That, for a fantasy and trick of fame,[4]
Go to their graves like beds, fight for a plot
Whereon the numbers cannot try the cause,
Which is not tomb enough and continent[5]
To hide the slain ?   O, from this time forth,
My thoughts be bloody, or be nothing worth !   [*Exit.*

SCENE V. *Elsinore.   A Room in the Castle.*

Enter QUEEN, HORATIO, *and a* Gentleman.

Queen. I will not speak with her.

Gentleman. She is importunate, indeed distract :[6]
Her mood will needs be pitied.

Queen.   What would she have ?

Gentleman. She speaks much of her father ; says she hears
There's tricks i' the world ; and hems, and beats her heart ;

---

[1] Animated.

[2] Cause of quarrel.   [3] Passion.

[4] " Fantasy and trick of fame," i.e., a deceptive appearance promising fame.

[5] That which contains ; receptacle.   [6] Distracted.

Spurns enviously [1] at straws; speaks things in doubt,
That carry but half sense: her speech is nothing,
Yet the unshaped use of it doth move
The hearers to collection; [2] they aim [3] at it,
And botch [4] the words up fit to their own thoughts;
Which, as her winks and nods and gestures yield them,
Indeed would make one think there might be thought,
Though nothing sure, yet much unhappily.

Horatio. 'Twere good she were spoken with; for she may strew
Dangerous conjectures in ill-breeding minds.

Queen. Let her come in.   [*Exit Horatio.*
To my sick soul, as sin's true nature is,
Each toy [5] seems prologue [6] to some great amiss: [7]
So full of artless jealousy [8] is guilt,
It spills itself in fearing to be spilt.

                    Reënter HORATIO, *with* OPHELIA.

Ophelia. Where is the beauteous Majesty of Denmark?
Queen. How now, Ophelia?

Ophelia. [Sings] *How should I your true love know*
                              From another one?
                         By his cockle hat and staff,
                              And his sandal shoon. [9]

Queen. Alas, sweet lady! what imports this song?
Ophelia. Say you? nay, pray you, mark.   [*Sings.*

---

[1] "Spurns enviously," i.e., kicks out spitefully at trifling objects in her path.

[2] "To collection," i.e., to attempt to put (her speech) into form.

[3] Guess.   [4] Patch.   [5] Trifle.

[6] Introduction.   [7] Misfortune.

[8] Suspicion.

[9] "Cockle hat," etc. This is a description of the pilgrim. The shell worn in his hat indicated that he had been, or was going, beyond seas (to the Holy Land). "Shoon" is the old plural of "shoe," a form that was archaic, however, in the Elizabethan age.

> *He is dead and gone, lady,*
> *He is dead and gone :*
> *At his head a grass-green turf,*
> *At his heels a stone.*

Queen. Nay, but, Ophelia,—

Ophelia. Pray you, mark.   -[*Sings.*

> *White his shroud as the mountain snow,*

Enter KING.

Queen. Alas ! look here, my lord.

Ophelia. [*Sings*]   *Larded with sweet flowers ;*
> *Which bewept to the grave did go*
> *With truelove showers.*

King. How do you, pretty lady ?

Ophelia. Well, God 'ild you ! [1] They say the owl was a baker's daughter.[2]   Lord, we know what we are, but know not what we may be.   God be at your table !

King. Conceit upon her father.

Ophelia.   Pray you, let's have no words of this; but when they ask you what it means, say you this :—   [*Sings.*

> *To-morrow is Saint Valentine's Day,*[3]
> *All in the morning betime,*
> *And I a maid at your window,*
> *To be your Valentine.*

King. How long has she been thus ?

Ophelia. I hope all will be well.   We must be patient; but I cannot choose but weep, to think they should lay him i' the cold

---

1 " 'Ild you," i.e., reward you.

2 There was an old legendary story current in England, that our Saviour was refused bread by a baker's daughter, who, for her want of charity, was transformed into an owl.

3 " This song alludes to the custom of the first girl seen by a man on the morning of this day [St. Valentine's Day] being considered his valentine,

ground.   My brother shall know of it; and so I thank you for
your good counsel.—Come, my coach!—Good night, ladies;
good night, sweet ladies; good night, good night.   [*Exit.*

   King.   Follow her close; give her good watch, I pray you.
                                       [*Exit Horatio.*

O, this is the poison of deep grief; it springs
All from her father's death.   O Gertrude, Gertrude!
When sorrows come, they come not single spies,
But in battalions.   First, her father slain;
Next, your son gone; and he most violent author
Of his own just remove: the people muddied,
Thick, and unwholesome in their thoughts and whispers,
For good Polonius' death; and we have done but greenly,[1]
In hugger-mugger[2] to inter him: poor Ophelia
Divided from herself and her fair judgment,[3]
Without the which we are pictures, or mere beasts;
Last, and as much containing[4] as all these,
Her brother is in secret come from France;
Feeds on his wonder, keeps himself in clouds,[5]
And wants not buzzers to infect his ear
With pestilent speeches of his father's death;
Wherein necessity, of matter beggar'd,
Will nothing stick our person to arraign
In ear and ear.   O my dear Gertrude! this,
Like to a murdering-piece,[6] in many places
Gives me superfluous death.   [*A noise within.*

or truelove. The custom of the different sexes choosing themselves mates on
St. Valentine's Day (14th of February), the names being selected either by lot
or by methods of divination, is of great antiquity in England."—HALLIWELL.

  1 Unwisely.

  2 "In hugger-mugger," i.e., in a hurried and stealthy manner.

  3 "Divided from herself," etc., i.e., beside herself; out of her senses.

  4 "As much containing," i.e., of as much importance.

  5 "Feeds on his wonder," etc., i.e., is full of doubt and amazement, and
keeps himself in gloomy reserve and suspicion.

  6 "Murdering-piece" was a cannon loaded with canister shot. This was

Queen.   Alack ! what noise is this ?

King. Where are my Switzers ?[1] Let them guard the door.—

Enter another Gentleman.

What is the matter ?

Gentleman.   Save yourself, my lord :

The ocean, overpeering of his list,[2]

Eats not the flats[3] with more impetuous haste

Than young Laertes, in a riotous head,[4]

O'erbears your officers.   The rabble call him lord ;

And, as the world were now but to begin,

Antiquity forgot, custom not known,

The ratifiers and props of every word,

They cry, " Choose we : Laertes shall be King !"

Caps, hands, and tongues applaud it to the clouds :

" Laertes shall be King, Laertes King !"

Queen. How cheerfully on the false trail they cry !

O, this is counter,[5] you false Danish dogs !

King. The doors are broke.   [*Noise within*

Enter LAERTES, *armed;* Danes *following.*

Laertes. Where is this King ?—Sirs, stand you all without.

Danes. No, let's come in.

Laertes.   I pray you, give me leave.

Danes. We will, we will.   [*They retire without the door.*

a case filled with bullets, nails, scraps of iron, etc., which, on striking its
mark when discharged from the gun, burst, and scattered the contents.

[1] Swiss mercenary soldiers were favorite bodyguards of the kings of Europe
in Shakespeare's time.   Malone, quoting Nash's Christ's Tears over Jerusa-
lem, published in 1594, says, " Law, logicke, and the Switzers may be hired
to fight for anybody."

[2] " Overpeering of his list," i.e., overflowing its limits.

[3] " Eats not the flats," i.e., submerges not the level beach.

[4] Armed band.

[5] " Counter," as a hunting term, means " tracing the scent backward."

Laertes. I thank you: keep the door.— O thou vile King,
Give me my father!

Queen.   Calmly, good Laertes.

Laertes. That drop of blood that's calm proclaims me bas-
    tard.

King. What is the cause, Laertes,
That thy rebellion looks so giant-like?—
Let him go, Gertrude; do not fear our person:
There's such divinity doth hedge [1] a king,
That treason can but peep to what it would,
Acts little of his will.— Tell me, Laertes,
Why thou art thus incens'd.— Let him go, Gertrude.—
Speak, man.

Laertes. Where is my father?

King.   Dead.

Queen.   But not by him.

King. Let him demand his fill.

Laertes. How came he dead? I'll not be juggled with.
To hell, allegiance! vows, to the blackest devil!
Conscience and grace,[2] to the profoundest pit!
I dare damnation. To this point I stand,
That both the worlds [3] I give to negligence,
Let come what comes; only I'll be reveng'd
Most throughly [4] for my father.

King.   Who shall stay you?

Laertes. My will, not all the world;
And for my means, I'll husband them so well,
They shall go far with little.

King.   Good Laertes,
If you desire to know the certainty
Of your dear father's death, is't writ in your revenge,

1 Surround.
2 Religion; religious feeling.
3 " Both the worlds," i.e., this world and the world to come.
4 Thoroughly.

That, swoopstake,[1] you will draw both friend and foe,
Winner and loser ?

    Laertes. None but his enemies.

    King.   Will you know them, then ?

    Laertcs. To his good friends thus wide I'll ope my arms ;
And like the kind life-rend'ring pelican,[2]
Repast them with my blood.

    King.   Why, now you speak
Like a good child and a true gentleman.
That I am guiltless of your father's death,
And am most sensibly in grief for it,
It shall as level to your judgment pierce
As day does to your eye.

    Danes.   [*Within*] Let her come in.

    Laertes. How now ! what noise is that ? —

Reënter OPHELIA.

O heat, dry up my brains ! tears seven times salt,
Burn out the sense and virtue of mine eye ! —
By Heaven, thy madness shall be paid with weight,
Till our scale turn the beam. O rose of May !
Dear maid, kind sister, sweet Ophelia ! —
O heavens ! is't possible a young maid's wits
Should be as mortal as an old man's life ?
Nature is fine in love, and where 'tis fine
It sends some precious instance [3] of itself
After the thing it loves.

---

[1] Sweepstake; a gambling term, meaning " to gather in all the stakes."

[2] This has reference to the old fable, that the pelican pierces her own breast to give sustenance to her young. Dr. Sherwen, as cited by Caldecott in a note quoted by Furness, thus accounts for the origin of the fable : " By the pelican's dropping upon her breast her lower bill to enable her young to take food from its capacious pouch, lined with fine flesh-colored skin, this appearance is, on feeding them, given."

[3] Sample.

Ophelia. [Sings] *They bore him barefac'd on the bier:*
                    Hey non nonny, nonny, hey nonny;
                    And in his grave rain'd many a tear.

Fare you well, my dove!

Laertes. Hadst thou thy wits, and didst persuade revenge,
It could not move thus.

Ophelia. [Sings] *You must sing a-down a-down,*
                    An you call him a-down-a.

O, how the wheel [1] becomes it!   It is the false steward that stole
his master's daughter.

Laertes. This nothing's more than matter.[2]

Ophelia. There's rosemary, that's for remembrance; pray, love,
remember: and there is pansies, that's for thoughts.

Laertes. A document [3] in madness; thoughts and remembrance
fitted.

Ophelia. There's fennel for you, and columbines: there's rue
for you; and here's some for me: we may call it herb-grace o'
Sundays: O, you must wear your rue with a difference. There's
a daisy: I would give you some violets,[4] but they wither'd all
when my father died. They say he made a good end— [*Sings.*

          For bonnie sweet Robin is all my joy.

Laertes. Thought and affliction, passion, hell itself,
She turns to favor and to prettiness.

Ophelia. [Sings] *And will he not come again?*
                    And will he not come again?
                    No, no, he is dead:
                    Go to thy deathbed,
                    He never will come again.

---

[1] Chorus, or burden.
[2] Meaning.   [3] A teaching; a lesson.
[4] "There's fennel," etc. Fennel is emblematic of flattery columbine of
ingratitude, and rue of sorrow. The violet is for faithfulness, and the
daisy signifies dissimulation.

> *His beard was as white as snow,*
> *All flaxen was his poll:* [1]
> *He is gone, he is gone,*
> *And we cast away moan:* [2]
> *God ha' mercy on his soul!*

And of all Christian souls, I pray God.   God be wi' ye.   [*Exit.*

Laertes.   Do you see this, O God?

King.   Laertes, I must com'mune [3] with your grief,
Or you deny me right.   Go but apart,
Make choice of whom your wisest friends you will,
And they shall hear and judge 'twixt you and me.
If by direct or by collateral hand
They find us touch'd, [4] we will our kingdom give,
Our crown, our life, and all that we call ours,
To you in satisfaction; but if not,
Be you content to lend your patience to us,
And we shall jointly labor with your soul
To give it due content.

Laertes.   Let this be so:
His means of death, his ob'scure funeral, —
No trophy, sword, nor hatchment [5] o'er his bones,
No noble rite nor formal ostentation, —
Cry to be heard, as 'twere from heaven to earth,
That I must call't in question.

King.   So you shall;
And where the offense is let the great ax fall.
I pray you, go with me.   [*Exeunt.*

---

[1] Head.

[2] " We cast away moan," i.e., waste our mourning.

[3] Make common cause.

[4] Implicated (in the murder of your father).

[5] " No trophy," etc.: " Not only the sword, but the helmet, gantlet, spurs, and tabard (i.e., a coat whereon the armorial bearings were anciently depicted, from whence the term ' coat of armor') are hung over the grave of every knight." — SIR J. HAWKINS.

SCENE VI. *Another Room in the Castle.*

Enter HORATIO *and a* Servant.

Horatio. What are they that would speak with me?
Servant. Sailors, sir.   They say they have letters for you.
Horatio. Let them come in.					[*Exit Servant*
I do not know from what part of the world
I should be greeted, if not from Lord Hamlet.

Enter Sailors.

First Sailor. God bless you, sir.
Horatio. Let him bless thee too.
First Sailor. He shall, sir, an't please him.   There's a letter for
you, sir,—it comes from the ambassador that was bound for England,—if your name be Horatio, as I am let to know [1] it is.

Horatio. [Reads] *"Horatio, when thou shalt have overlook'd
this, give these fellows some means [2] to the King: they have letters for
him.   Ere we were two days old at sea, a pirate of very warlike appointment [3] gave us chase.   Finding ourselves too slow of sail, we put
on a compelled [4] valor, and in the grapple I boarded them: on the
instant [5] they got clear of our ship, so I alone became their prisoner.
They have dealt with me like thieves of mercy: but they knew what
they did; I am to do a good turn for them.   Let the King have the
letters I have sent; and repair thou to me with as much speed as thou
wouldst fly death.   I have words to speak in thine ear will make thee
dumb; yet are they much too light for the bore of the matter. [6]   These
good fellows will bring thee where I am.   Rosencrantz and Guildenstern
hold their course for England: of them I have much to tell thee.
Farewell.*

                    "He that thou knowest thine, HAMLET."

---

  [1] " Let to know," i.e., informed.
  [2] Means of access.		[3] Equipment.		[4] Enforced.
  [5] " On the instant," i.e., at the moment.
  [6] " For the bore of the matter:" " The bore is the caliber of a gun, or the
capacity of the barrel. 'The matter,' says Hamlet, 'would carry heavier
words.'"—JOHNSON.

Come, I will make you way for these your letters;
And do't the speedier, that you may direct me
To him from whom you brought them.   [*Exeunt.*

Scene VII.   *Another Room in the Castle.*

Enter King *and* Laertes.

King. Now must your conscience my acquitance seal,
And you must put me in your heart for friend,
Sith you have heard, and with a knowing ear,
That he which hath your noble father slain
Pursu'd my life.
Laertes.   It well appears; but tell me
Why you proceeded not against these feats,
So crimeful [1] and so capital in nature,
As by your safety, wisdom, all things else,
You mainly were stirr'd up.
King.   O, for two special reasons,
Which may to you, perhaps, seem much unsinew'd, [2]
But yet to me they are strong. The Queen, his mother,
Lives almost by his looks; and for myself,—
My virtue or my plague, be it either which,—
She's so conjunctive to my life and soul, [3]
That, as the star moves not but in his sphere,
I could not but by her. The other motive
Why to a public count I might not go,
Is the great love the general gender [4] bear him;
Who, dipping all his faults in their affection,
Would, like the spring that turneth wood to stone,
Convert his gyves to graces; [5] so that my arrows,

---

[1] Heinous.   [2] " Much unsinew'd," i.e., of little force.
[3] " So conjunctive to my life and soul," i.e., so much a part of me.
[4] " The general gender," i.e., the masses; the common people.
[5] " Convert his gyves to graces," i.e., " were I to put him in bonds, the
fetters would only give him a more general favor."— Moberly.

Too slightly timber'd for so loud a wind,[1]
Would have reverted to my bow again,
And not where I had aim'd them.

    Laertes. And so have I a noble father lost;
A sister driven into desperate terms,
Whose worth, if praises may go back again,[2]
Stood challenger on mount of all the age
For her perfections. But my revenge will come.

    King. Break not your sleeps for that: you must not think
That we are made of stuff so flat and dull,
That we can let our beard be shook with danger,
And think it pastime. You shortly shall hear more:
I lov'd your father, and we love ourself;
And that, I hope, will teach you to imagine —

Enter a Messenger.

How now ! what news ?

    Messenger.   Letters, my lord, from Hamlet.
This to your Majesty; this to the Queen.

    King. From Hamlet ! who brought them ?

    Messenger. Sailors, my lord, they say; I saw them not.
They were given me by Claudio; he receiv'd them
Of him that brought them.

    King.   Laertes, you shall hear them. —
Leave us.   *[Exit Messenger.*

[Reads] *"High and mighty, You shall know I am set naked on
your kingdom. To-morrow shall I beg leave to see your kingly eyes;
when I shall, first asking your pardon thereunto, recount the occasion
of my sudden and more strange return.*

" HAMLET."

What should this mean ? Are all the rest come back ?
Or is it some abuse,[3] and no such thing ?

---

  [1] " Too slightly timber'd," etc. Steevens quotes from Ascham's Toxoph-
ilus : " Weake bowes and lyghte shaftes cannot stande in a rough wynde."
  [2] " If praises may go back again," i.e., if I may praise what has been, but
is now to be found no more.   [3] Deception.

Laertes. Know you the hand?

King.   'Tis Hamlet's character.[1]   " Naked ! "
And in a postscript here, he says " alone."
Can you advise me?

Laertes. I'm lost in it,[2] my lord.   But let him come:
It warms the very sickness in my heart,
That I shall live and tell him to his teeth,
" Thus didest thou."

King.   If it be so, Laertes, —
As how should it be so? how otherwise? —
Will you be rul'd by me?

Laertes.   Ay, my lord;
So you will not o'errule me to a peace.

King. To thine own peace.   If he be now return'd, —
As checking[3] at his voyage, and that he means
No more to undertake it, — I will work him
To an exploit, now ripe in my device,
Under the which he shall not choose but fall;
And for his death no wind of blame shall breathe,[4]
But even his mother shall uncharge the practice,[5]
And call it accident.

Laertes.   My lord, I will be rul'd;
The rather, if you could devise it so
That I might be the organ.

King.   It falls right.
You have been talk'd of since your travel much,
And that in Hamlet's hearing, for a quality
Wherein, they say, you shine: your sum of parts

---

1 Handwriting.

2 " I'm lost in it," i.e., I can make nothing of it; do not understand it.

3 Turning back, or away from. The phrase is from falconry. The hawk
" checks " when it flies off or away from pursuit of the game.

4 " And for his death no wind of blame shall breathe," i.e., for his death,
there shall be no suspicion of blame.

5 " Uncharge the practice," i.e., make no charge or accusation of a
plot.

Did not together pluck such envy from him
As did that one, and that, in my regard, .
Of the unworthiest siege.¹

    Laertes.   What part is that, my lord ?

    King. A very riband in the cap of youth,²
Yet needful too; for youth no less becomes
The light and careless livery that it wears
Than settled age his sables and his weeds,
Importing health and graveness.   Two months since,
Here was a gentleman of Normandy.
I've seen myself, and serv'd against, the French,
And they can well on horseback:³ but this gallant
Had witchcraft in't; he grew unto his seat;
And to such wondrous doing brought his horse,
As had he been incorps'd and demi-natur'd
With the brave beast:⁴ so far he topp'd ⁵ my thought,
That I, in forgery of shapes and tricks,⁶
Came short of what he did.

    Laertes.   A Norman was't ?

    King. A Norman.

    Laertes. Upon my life, Lamond.

    King.   The very same.

    Laertes. I know him well: he is the brooch indeed
And gem of all the nation.

    King. He made confession of you,⁷
And gave you such a masterly report ⁸

---

1 " Unworthiest siege," i.e., least worthy sort or kind.

2 " A very riband," etc., i.e., a mere youthful ornament.

3 " Can well on horseback," i.e., can do well; are good riders.

4 " As had he been," etc., i.e., as though he and his noble steed were one and the same animal.

5 Went beyond.

6 " That I, in forgery of shapes and tricks," i.e., that anything I had imagined of feats (of horsemanship).

7 " Made confession of you," i.e., admitted your excellence.

8 " Masterly report," i.e., report of masterly skill.

For art and exercise in your defense,[1]
And for your rapier most especially,
That he cried out, 'twould be a sight indeed
If one could match you: the scrimers[2] of their nation,
He swore, had neither motion, guard, nor eye,
If you oppos'd them.   Sir, this report of his
Did Hamlet so envenom with his envy,
That he could nothing do but wish and beg
Your sudden coming o'er, to play with him.
Now, out of this,—

    Laertes.   What out of this, my lord ?
    King.   Laertes, was your father dear to you ?
Or are you like the painting of a sorrow,
A face without a heart ?
    Laertes.   Why ask you this ?
    King.   Not that I think you did not love your father;
But that I know love is begun by time,
And that I see, in passages of proof,[3]
Time qualifies the spark and fire of it.
There lives within the very flame of love
A kind of wick or snuff that will abate it;
And nothing is at a like goodness still;
For goodness, growing to a plurisy,[4]
Dies in his own too-much.   That we would do,
We should do when we would; for this "would" changes,
And hath abatements and delays as many
As there are tongues, are hands, are accidents;
And then this "should" is like a spendthrift sigh,[5]
That hurts by easing.   But, to the quick o' the ulcer:[6]

---

[1] Self-defense; use of sword, rapier, etc.   [2] Fencers.
[3] "Passages of proof," i.e., instances to prove it.   [4] Fullness.
[5] "Spendthrift sigh," i.e., a wasting sigh.   It is an old superstition that sighs impair the strength, and wear out the animal powers.
[6] "But, to the quick o' the ulcer," i.e., to come to the main point of this business.

Hamlet comes back: what would you undertake,
To show yourself your father's son in deed
More than in words?

Laertes.   To cut his throat i' the church.

King. No place, indeed, should murder sanctuarize;[1]
Revenge should have no bounds.   But, good Laertes,
Will you do this, keep close within your chamber.
Hamlet return'd shall know you are come home:
We'll put on those shall praise your excellence,
And set a double varnish on the fame
The Frenchman gave you; bring you in fine[2] together,
And wager on your heads.   He, being remiss,[3]
Most generous, and free from all contriving,
Will not peruse[4] the foils; so that, with ease,
Or with a little shuffling, you may choose
A sword unbated,[5] and in a pass of practice[6]
Requite him for your father.

Laertes.   I will do't;
And for that purpose I'll anoint my sword.
I bought an unction of a mountebank,
So mortal, that, but dip a knife in it,
Where it draws blood no cataplasm so rare,
Collected from all simples[7] that have virtue
Under the moon, can save the thing from death

---

1 This word "sanctuarize" does not appear elsewhere. The reference, however, is to an old law of England, which has been greatly modified from time to time by acts of Parliament, under which a person committing any crime, — except treason and sacrilege, — and taking refuge in a church, church-yard, or other specified sanctuary, could save his life, if, within forty days thereafter, he confessed his guilt to the coroner, and observed other conditions, one of which was to leave the country forthwith.

2 "Bring you in fine," i.e., in the end bring you.

3 Indifferent.   4 Examine.

5 Without a button on its point.

6 "A pass of practice," i.e., a treacherous thrust · a pass made with this foil, as though ignorant of its being "unbated."   7 Herbs.

That is but scratch'd withal: I'll touch my point
With this contagion, that, if I gall him slightly,
It may be death.

King.   Let's further think of this;
Weigh what convenience both of time and means
May fit us to our shape.   If this should fail,
And that our drift look through [1] our bad performance,
'Twere better not assay'd: therefore this project
Should have a back, or second, that might hold,
If this should blast in proof.   Soft ! let me see;
We'll make a solemn wager on your cunnings.
I ha't: [2]
When in your motion you are hot and dry, —
As make your bouts [3] more violent to that end, —
And that he calls for drink, I'll have prepar'd him
A chalice [4] for the nonce, [5] whereon but sipping,
If he by chance escape your venom'd stuck, [6]
Our purpose may hold there. —

Enter QUEEN.

                    How now, sweet Queen !
Queen.   One woe doth tread upon another's heel,
So fast they follow. — Your sister's drown'd, Laertes.

Laertes.   Drown'd !   O, where ?

Queen.   There is a willow grows aslant [7] a brook,
That shows his hoar leaves in the glassy stream;
There with fantastic garlands did she come,
Of crowflowers, nettles, daisies, and long purples.
There, on the pendent boughs her coronet weeds [8]

[1] " Our drift look through," i.e., our purpose be discovered.
[2] Have it.   [3] Heats, or turns.   [4] Cup.
[5] " For the nonce," i.e., for the occasion; for the once.
[6] " Your venom'd stuck," i.e., thrust of your poisoned foil.
[7] Bending over.
[8] " Coronet weeds," i.e., the flowers she had formed into a crown, or chaplet.

Clambering to hang, an envious sliver [1] broke;
When down her weedy trophies and herself
Fell in the weeping brook.   Her clothes spread wide,
And, mermaid-like, a while they bore her up;
Which time she chanted snatches [2] of old tunes,
As one incapable [3] of her own distress,
Or like a creature native and indued [4]
Unto that element: but long it could not be
Till that her garments, heavy with their drink,
Pull'd the poor wretch [5] from her melodious lay
To muddy death.

　　Laertes.　　　　　Alas ! then, she is drown'd ?
　　Queen. Drown'd, drown'd.
　　Laertes. Too much of water hast thou, poor Ophelia,
And therefore I forbid my tears.   But yet
It is our trick; [6] nature her custom holds,
Let shame say what it will: when these are gone,
The woman will be out.— Adieu, my lord;
I have a speech of fire, that fain would blaze,
But that this folly douts it. [7]　　　　　　　　　[*Exit.*

　　King.　　　　　　Let's follow, Gertrude.
How much I had to do to calm his rage !
Now fear I this will give it start again;
Therefore let's follow.　　　　　　　　　　[*Exeunt.*

ACT V.

SCENE I.　*A Churchyard.*

Enter two Clowns, *with spades, etc.*

　First Clown. Is she to be buried in Christian burial that willfully seeks her own salvation ?

　Second Clown. I tell thee she is; and therefore make her

---

[1] Small branch.　　　[2] Scraps.　　　[3] Insensible.　　　[4] Suited.
[5] See Note 3, p. 63.　　　[6] Habit.　　　[7] See Note 2, p. 43.

grave straight:[1] the crowner [2] hath sat on her, and finds it [3] Christian burial.

First Clown. How can that be, unless she drown'd herself in her own defense?

Second Clown. Why, 'tis found so.

First Clown. It must be *se offendendo ;* [4] it cannot be else. For here lies the point: if I drown myself wittingly, it argues an act; and an act hath three branches; it is, to act, to do, and to perform: argal, she drown'd herself wittingly.

Second Clown. Nay, but hear you, goodman delver.

First Clown. Give me leave. Here lies the water; good: here stands the man; good: if the man go to this water and drown himself, it is, will he, nill he, he goes,— mark you that; but if the water come to him and drown him, he drowns not himself: argal, he that is not guilty of his own death shortens not his own life.

Second Clown. But is this law?

First Clown. Ay, marry, is't; crowner's quest [5] law.

Second Clown. Will you ha' the truth on't? If this had not been a gentlewoman, she should have been buried out o' Christian burial.

First Clown. Why, there thou say'st; and the more pity that great folk should have countenance in this world to drown or hang themselves, more than their even Christian.[6] Come, my spade. There is no ancient gentlemen but gardeners, ditchers, and gravemakers; they hold up Adam's profession.

Second Clown. Was he a gentleman?

First Clown. A'[7] was the first that ever bore arms.

Second Clown. Why, he had none.

---

[1] See Note 2, p. 104.   [2] Coroner.

[3] "Finds it," i.e., decides it.

[4] The gravedigger would have said *se deffendendo* (Latin: "self-defense"); and two or three lines below he has *argal* for the Latin *ergo* ("therefore").

[5] Inquest.   [6] Fellow-Christian.

[7] A colloquial abbreviation of "he," often met with in old plays.

First Clown. What, art a heathen? How dost thou understand the Scripture? The Scripture says, "Adam digg'd:" could he dig without arms? I'll put another question to thee: if thou answerest me not to the purpose, confess thyself —

Second Clown. Go to.[1]

First Clown. What is he that builds stronger than either the mason, the shipwright, or the carpenter?

Second Clown. The gallowsmaker; for that frame outlives a thousand tenants.

First Clown. I like thy wit well, in good faith: the gallows does well; but how does it well? it does well to those that do ill: now thou dost ill to say the gallows is built stronger than the church: argal, the gallows may do well to thee. To't again, come.

Second Clown. "Who builds stronger than a mason, a shipwright, or a carpenter?"

First Clown. Ay, tell me that, and unyoke.[2]

Second Clown. Marry, now I can tell.

First Clown. To't.

Second Clown. Mass, I cannot tell.

Enter HAMLET *ana* HORATIO, *at a distance.*

First Clown. Cudgel thy brains no more about it, for your dull ass will not mend his pace with beating; and, when you are ask'd this question next, say, "a gravemaker:" the houses that he makes last till doomsday. Go, get thee to Yaughan: fetch me a stoup[3] of liquor.   [*Exit Second Clown.*
                    [*First Clown digs, and sings.*

> *In youth, when I did love, did love,*
>   *Methought it was very sweet,*
> *To contract, O![4] the time, for, ah! my behove,*
>   *O, methought, there was nothing meet.*

1 Come on (see Note 3, p. 40).   2 Quit.   3 Flagon.
4 The "O's" and "ah's" in the lines the clown sings are no part of the song, but represent his forced breathing as he strikes with his mattock in digging.

Hamlet. Has this fellow no feeling of his business, that he sings at gravemaking?

Horatio. Custom hath made it in him a property of easiness.

Hamlet. 'Tis e'en so: the hand of little employment hath the daintier sense.[1]

First Clown. [Sings]

> *But age, with his stealing steps,*
> *Hath claw'd me in his clutch,*
> *And hath shipp'd me intil the land,*
> *As if I had never been such.*

[*Throws up a skull.*

Hamlet. That skull had a tongue in it, and could sing once: how the knave jowls[2] it to the ground, as if it were Cain's jaw-bone, that did the first murder! It might be the pate of a politician,[3] which this ass now o'erreaches; one that would circumvent God, might it not?

Horatio. It might, my lord.

Hamlet. Or of a courtier, which could say, "Good morrow, sweet lord! How dost thou, good lord?" This might be my Lord Such-a-one, that prais'd my Lord Such-a-one's horse, when he meant to beg it, might it not?

Horatio. Ay, my lord.

Hamlet. Why, e'en so; and now my Lady Worm's, chapless, and knock'd about the mazzard[4] with a sexton's spade. Here's fine revolution, and we had the trick to see't. Did these bones cost no more the breeding, but to play at loggats[5] with 'em? mine ache to think on't.

---

[1] "Hath the daintier sense," i.e., is the more delicately sensitive.

[2] Dashes; throws rudely.

[3] Schemer. Shakespeare always uses the word "politician" in a bad sense.

[4] Skull.

[5] A game played on a floor strewed with ashes. The jack, or mark, was a wheel made of hard wood; the loggat, of which each player had three, was a truncated cone, held tightly at the thin end; and the object was to pitch them so as to lie as nearly as possible to the jack.

First Clown. [Sings]

> *A pickax, and a spade, a spade,*
> *For and a shrouding sheet:*
> *O, a pit of clay for to be made*
> *For such a guest is meet.*

                                   [Throws up another skull.

Hamlet. There's another: why may not that be the skull of a lawyer? Where be his quiddities now, his quillets,[1] his cases, his tenures, and his tricks? why does he suffer this rude knave now to knock him about the sconce[2] with a dirty shovel, and will not tell him of his action of battery? Hum! This fellow might be in's time a great buyer of land, with his statutes, his recognizances, his fines, his double vouchers, his recoveries:[3] is this the fine of his fines, and the recovery of his recoveries, to have his fine pate full of fine dirt? will his vouchers vouch him no more of his purchases, and double ones too, than the length and breadth of a pair of indentures?[4] The very conveyances[5] of his lands will hardly lie in this box; and must the inheritor himself have no more, ha?

Horatio. Not a jot more, my lord.

Hamlet. Is not parchment made of sheepskins?

Horatio. Ay, my lord, and of calfskins too.

---

1 "Quiddities" and "quillets," i.e., nice, hair-drawn distinctions and subtilties; generally applied to the subtilties of lawyers.

2 Head.

3 "His statutes," etc.: Lord Campbell, as quoted by Furness, remarks that "these terms of art are all used seemingly with a full knowledge of their import, and it would puzzle some practicing barristers with whom I am acquainted to go over the whole in regular order and to define each of them satisfactorily."

4 This instrument of writing, "a pair of indentures," is thus described by Sir William Blackstone: "If a deed be made by more parties than one, there ought to be regularly as many copies of it as there are parties, and each should be cut or *indented* (formerly in acute angles, like the teeth of a saw, but at present in waving lines) on the top or side, to tally or correspond with each other; which deed, so made, is called an *indenture.*"

5 Title deeds.

Hamlet. They are sheep and calves which seek out assurance [1] in that. I will speak to this fellow. — Whose grave's this, sirrah?

First Clown. Mine, sir.   [*Sings.*

> *O, a pit of clay for to be made*
> *For such a guest is meet.*

Hamlet. I think it be thine, indeed; for thou liest in't.

First Clown. You lie out on't, sir, and therefore it is not yours: for my part, I do not lie in't, and yet it is mine.

Hamlet. Thou dost lie in't, to be in't and say it is thine: 'tis for the dead, not for the quick;[2] therefore thou liest.

First Clown. 'Tis a quick lie, sir: 'twill away again, from me to you.

Hamlet. What man dost thou dig it for?

First Clown. For no man, sir.

Hamlet. What woman, then?

First Clown. For none, neither.

Hamlet. Who's to be buried in't?

First Clown. One that was a woman, sir; but, rest her soul, she's dead.

Hamlet. How absolute [3] the knave is! we must speak by the card,[4] or equivocation will undo us. By the Lord, Horatio, these three years I have taken note of it: the age is grown so picked,[5] that the toe of the peasant comes so near the heel of the courtier, he galls his kibe.[6] — How long hast thou been a gravemaker?

First Clown. Of all the days i' the year, I come to't that day that our last King Hamlet overcame Fortinbras.

Hamlet. How long is that since?

First Clown. Cannot you tell that? every fool can tell that. It was the very day that young Hamlet was born; he that is mad, and sent into England.

---

[1] Deeds, usually written on parchment, are called "assurances."

[2] "The quick," i.e., the living.   [3] Positive.

[4] "By the card," i.e., with the utmost precision.   [5] Smart.

[6] "Galls his kibe," i.e., chafes his chilblain.

Hamlet. Ay, marry, why was he sent into England ?

First Clown. Why, because he was mad : he shall recover his wits there; or, if he do not, it's no great matter there.

Hamlet. Why ?

First Clown. 'Twill not be seen in him there : there the men are as mad as he.

Hamlet. How came he mad ?

First Clown. Very strangely, they say.

Hamlet. How strangely ?

First Clown. Faith, e'en with losing his wits.

Hamlet. Upon what ground ?

First Clown. Why, here in Denmark : I have been sexton here, man and boy, thirty years.

Hamlet. How long will a man lie i' the earth ere he rot ?

First Clown. I' faith, if he be not rotten before he die, — as we have many pocky corses nowadays that will scarce hold the laying in, — he will last you some eight year or nine year : a tanner will last you nine year.

Hamlet. Why he more than another ?

First Clown. Why, sir, his hide is so tann'd with his trade, that he will keep out water a great while; and your water is a sore decayer of your dead body. Here's a skull now; this skull has lain in the earth three and twenty years.

Hamlet. Whose was it ?

First Clown. A jolly mad fellow's it was : whose do you think it was ?

Hamlet. Nay, I know not.

First Clown. A pestilence on him for a mad rogue ! a' poured a flagon of Rhenish [1] on my head once. This same skull, sir, was Yorick's skull, the King's jester.

Hamlet. This ?

First Clown. E'en that.

Hamlet. Let me see. [*Takes the skull.*] Alas, poor Yorick ! — I knew him, Horatio : a fellow of infinite jest,[2] of most ex-

1 See Note 3, p. 42.   2 Wit.

cellent fancy : he hath borne me on his back a thousand times ; and now, how abhorred in my imagination it is ! my gorge rises at it.   Here hung those lips that I have kiss'd I know not how oft. — Where be your gibes now ? your gambols ? your songs ? your flashes of merriment, that were wont to set the table on [1] a roar ?   Not one now, to mock your own grinning ? quite chap-fallen ?   Now get you to my lady's chamber, and tell her, let her paint an inch thick, to this favor she must come ; make her laugh at that. — Prithee, Horatio, tell me one thing.

Horatio.   What's that, my lord ?

Hamlet.   Dost thou think Alexander look'd o' this fashion i' the earth ?

Horatio.   E'en so.

Hamlet.   And smelt so ? pah !   [*Puts down the skull.*

Horatio.   E'en so, my lord.

Hamlet.   To what base uses we may return, Horatio !   Why may not imagination trace the noble dust of Alexander till he find it stopping a bunghole ?

Horatio.   'Twere to consider too curiously,[2] to consider so.

Hamlet.   No, faith, not a jot ; but to follow him thither with modesty enough,[3] and likelihood to lead it ; as thus : Alexander died, Alexander was buried, Alexander returneth into dust ; the dust is earth ; of earth we make loam ; and why of that loam, whereto he was converted, might they not stop a beer barrel ?

Imperious [4] Cæsar, dead, and turn'd to clay,
Might stop a hole to keep the wind away :
O, that that earth, which kept the world in awe,
Should patch a wall to expel the winter's flaw ! [5]

But soft ! but soft ! aside :[6] here comes the King,

[1] In.   [2] Fancifully.
[3] " Modesty enough," i.e., without exaggeration.
[4] Imperial.
[5] Gust of wind.
[6] Step aside.

Enter Priests, *etc.*, *in procession ; the Corpse of* OPHELIA, LAERTES *and*
      Mourners *following ;* KING, QUEEN, *their Trains, etc.*

The Queen, the courtiers. Who is this they follow,
And with such maimed [1] rites ?   This doth betoken
The corse they follow did with desperate hand
Fordo [2] its own life: 'twas of some estate.[3]
Couch [4] we a while, and mark.   [*Retiring with Horatio.*

    Laertes. What ceremony else ?

    Hamlet.   That is Laertes,
A very noble youth: mark.

    Laertes. What ceremony else ?

    First Priest. Her obsequies [5] have been as far enlarg'd
As we have warranty: her death was doubtful;
And, but that great command o'ersways the order,[6]
She should in ground unsanctified have lodg'd
Till the last trumpet; for charitable prayers,
Shards,[7] flints, and pebbles should be thrown on her:
Yet here she is allow'd her virgin crants,[8]
Her maiden strewments, and the bringing home
Of bell and burial.[9]

    Laertes. Must there no more be done ?

    First Priest.   No more be done !
We should profane the service of the dead
To sing a requiem and such rest to her
As to peace-parted souls.

    Laertes.   Lay her i' the earth;
And from her fair and unpolluted flesh

---

  1 Imperfect.   2 See Note 3, p. 56.
  3 Rank.   4 Hide.
  5 Funeral ceremonies.
  6 " Great command o'ersways the order," i.e., the command or influence
of the King overbears the rule of the church.
  7 Broken pottery and other refuse.
  8 Garlands.
  9 " Maiden strewments," etc., i.e., the strewing of the grave with flowers,
and the funeral bell at her burial.

May violets spring ! — I tell thee, churlish priest,
A ministering angel shall my sister be,
When thou liest howling.

 Hamlet.   What, the fair Ophelia !
 Queen. Sweets to the sweet: farewell ! [*Scattering flowers.*
I hop'd thou shouldst have been my Hamlet's wife;
I thought thy bridebed to have deck'd, sweet maid,
And not t' have strew'd thy grave.

 Laertes.   O, treble woe
Fall ten times treble on that cursed head
Whose wicked deed thy most ingenious [1] sense
Depriv'd thee of ! — Hold off the earth a while,
Till I have caught her once more in mine arms.

           [*Leaps into the grave.*
Now pile your dust upon the quick [2] and dead,
Till of this flat a mountain you have made,
To o'ertop old Pelion or the skyish head
Of blue Olympus.[3]

 Hamlet. [*Advancing*] What is he whose grief
Bears such an emphasis? whose phrase of sorrow
Conjures the wand'ring stars,[4] and makes them stand
Like wonder-wounded [5] hearers? This is I,
Hamlet the Dane.   [*Leaps into the grave.*
 Laertes.   The devil take thy soul !

           [*Grappling with him*
 Hamlet. Thou pray'st not well.
I prithee, take thy fingers from my throat;

---

[1] Ready of comprehension.   [2] See Note 2, p. 142.
[3] Olympus is a lofty mountain of Thessaly, whose top was supposed by the ancients to touch the heavens; and " from that circumstance, they placed the residence of the gods there, and made it the court of Jupiter." The Titans, in their war with the gods, endeavored to reach their dwelling place by piling, the one upon the other, Pelion and Ossa, two other mountain peaks of the country.
[4] " Wand'ring stars," i.e., the planets in their course.
[5] Wonder-stricken.

For, though I am not splenitive [1] and rash,
Yet have I something in me dangerous,
Which let thy wisdom fear.   Hold off thy hand.

   King. Pluck them asunder.

   Queen.   Hamlet, Hamlet !

   All. Gentlemen—

   Horatio.   Good my lord, be quiet.

       [*The Attendants part them, and they come out of the grave.*

   Hamlet. Why, I will fight with him upon this theme
Until my eyelids will no longer wag.

   Queen. O my son, what theme ?

   Hamlet. I lov'd Ophelia : forty thousand brothers
Could not, with all their quantity of love,
Make up my sum. — What wilt thou do for her ?

   King. O, he is mad, Laertes.

   Queen. For love of God, forbear him.

   Hamlet. 'Swounds, show me what thou'lt do :
Woo't [2] weep ? woo't fight ? woo't fast ? woo't tear thyself ?
Woo't drink up eisel ? [3] eat a crocodile ?
I'll do't.   Dost thou come here to whine ?
To outface me with leaping in her grave ?
Be buried quick [4] with her, and so will I ;
And, if thou prate [5] of mountains, let them throw
Millions of acres on us, till our ground,
Singeing his pate against the burning zone,
Make Ossa [6] like a wart !   Nay, an thou'lt mouth, [7]
I'll rant as well as thou.

   Queen.   This is mere madness :
And thus a while the fit will work on him ;

---

[1] " Not splenitive," i.e., not suddenly moved to anger.
[2] Wouldst thou.
[3] " Drink up eisel," i.e., quaff down vinegar.
[4] Alive.   [5] Talk wildly.
[6] See Note 3, p. 146.
[7] " An thou'lt mouth," i.e., if thou wilt brag.

Anon, as patient as the female dove
When that her golden couplets are disclos'd,[1]
His silence will sit drooping.

    Hamlet.   Hear you, sir;
What is the reason that you use me thus ?
I lov'd you ever.   But it is no matter;
Let Hercules himself do what he may,
The cat will mew, and dog will have his day.[2]   [*Exit.*

    King. I pray you, good Horatio, wait upon him.

                                       [*Exit Horatio.*

[*To Laertes*] Strengthen your patience in our last night's speech;
We'll put the matter to the present push.[3]—
Good Gertrude, set some watch over your son.—
This grave shall have a living [4] monument:
An hour of quiet shortly shall we see;
Till then, in patience our proceeding be.   [*Exeunt.*

SCENE II.   *A Hall in the Castle.*

Enter HAMLET *and* HORATIO.

    Hamlet. So much for this, sir: now shall you see the other.
You do remember all the circumstance ?

    Horatio. Remember it, my lord !

    Hamlet. Sir, in my heart there was a kind of fighting,
That would not let me sleep: methought I lay
Worse than the mutines [5] in the bilboes.[6]   Rashly,—

---

  [1] Hatched.   The dove sits on two eggs ; and the nestlings, when hatched,
are covered with downy yellow feathers.

  [2] " Let Hercules," etc., i.e., nature will take its own course, and Hercules
himself, with all his strength, cannot turn it aside.

  [3] " Present push," i.e., immediate trial.

  [4] Enduring.   [5] Mutineers.

  [6] " The ' bilboes ' is a bar of iron with fetters annexed to it, by which muti-
nous or disorderly sailors were anciently linked together.   The word is derived
from Bilboa, a place in Spain where instruments of steel were fabricated in

And prais'd be rashness for it, — let us know,
Our indiscretion sometimes serves us well
When our deep plots do fail; and that should teach us
There's a divinity that shapes our ends,
Roughhew them how we will.

   Horatio.   That is most certain.

   Hamlet. Up from my cabin,
My sea gown scarf'd about me, in the dark
Grop'd I to find out them; had my desire;
Finger'd their packet, and in fine withdrew
To mine own room again; making so bold,
My fears forgetting manners, to unseal
Their grand commission; where I found, Horatio, —
O royal knavery ! — an exact command,
Larded with many several sorts of reasons
Importing [1] Denmark's health and England's too,
With, ho ! such bugs and goblins in my life,[2]
That, on the supervise, no leisure bated,[3]
No, not to stay the grinding of the ax,
My head should be struck off.

   Horatio.   Is't possible ?

   Hamlet. Here's the commission : read it at more leisure.
But wilt thou hear me how I did proceed ?

   Horatio. I beseech you.

   Hamlet. Being thus benetted round with villainies, —
Ere I could make a prologue to my brains,
They had begun the play, — I sat me down,
Devis'd a new commission, wrote it fair.

the utmost perfection. . . . As these fetters connect the legs of the offenders very close together, . . . every motion of one must disturb his partner in confinement." — STEEVENS and JOHNSON : *Shakespeare* (edition 1785).

  [1] Concerning.

  [2] " Bugs and goblins in my life," i.e., bugbear stories of threatened danger, were I allowed to live.

  [3] " On the supervise, no leisure bated," i.e., on reading the commission, without the least delay.

I once did hold it, as our statists [1] do,
A baseness to write fair, and labor'd much
How to forget that learning; but, sir, now
It did me yeoman's service.[2]   Wilt thou know
The effect of what I wrote?

   Horatio.   Ay, good my lord.

   Hamlet. An earnest conjuration from the King,
As England was his faithful tributary,
As love between them like the palm might flourish,
As peace should still her wheaten garland [3] wear,
And stand a comma [4] 'tween their amities,
And many such-like as's of great charge,[5]
That, on the view and knowing of these contents,
Without debatement further, more or less,
He should the bearers put to sudden death,
Not shriving time allow'd.[6]

   Horatio.   How was this seal'd?

   Hamlet. Why, even in that was Heaven ordinant.[7]
I had my father's signet in my purse,
Which was the model of that Danish seal;
Folded the writ [8] up in form of the other,
Subscrib'd it, gave't the impression, plac'd it safely,
The changeling [9] never known.   Now, the next day

[1] Statesmen.

[2] "Yeoman's service:" the yeomanry of England in old times were free-holders, well-to-do farmers, and were among the most serviceable of the King's troops.

[3] "Wheaten garland," since wheat is symbolical of peace and plenty.

[4] "The comma is the note of connection and continuity; the period is the note of abruption and disjunction."

[5] Weight.

[6] "Not shriving time allow'd," i.e., no time allowed to confess their sins.

[7] Provident.

[8] Commission.

[9] It was charged against the fairies that they would steal the well-formed and handsome babe from its cradle, and leave a deformed one in its place; and this was called a "changeling."

Was our sea fight; and what to this was sequent
Thou know'st already.

Horatio. So Guildenstern and Rosencrantz go to't.

Hamlet. Why, man, they did make love to this employment:
They are not near my conscience; their defeat
Does by their own insinuation grow.[1]
'Tis dangerous when the baser nature[2] comes
Between the pass and fell incensed points
Of mighty opposites.[3]

Horatio.   Why, what a king is this !

Hamlet. Does it not, think'st thee, stand me now upon[4] —
He that hath kill'd my king, and stain'd my mother,
Popp'd in between the election and my hopes,
Thrown out his angle[5] for my proper[6] life,
And with such cozenage — is't not perfect conscience,[7]
To quit[8] him with this arm ? and is't not to be damn'd,
To let this canker of our nature come
In[9] further evil ?

Horatio. It must be shortly known to him from England
What is the issue of the business there.

Hamlet. It will be short: the interim is mine;
And a man's life's no more than to say " One."
But I am very sorry, good Horatio,
That to Laertes I forgot myself;
For, by the image of my cause, I see
The portraiture of his.   I'll court his favors;

---

1 " Does by their own insinuation grow," i.e., comes from their having
willingly put themselves into the business.

2 " The baser nature," i.e., those inferior in rank and courage.

3 Opponents.

4 " Stand me now upon," i.e., become my unavoidable duty.

5 Hooked fishing line.

6 Very.

7 " Is't not perfect conscience," i.e., am I not clearly justifiable?

8 Requite.

9 Into.

But, sure, the bravery [1] of his grief did put me
Into a towering passion.

Horatio.　　　　　　　　Peace ! who comes here ?

Enter OSRIC.

Osric. Your lordship is right welcome back to Denmark.

Hamlet. I humbly thank you, sir. — Dost know this water-fly ?

Horatio. No, my good lord.

Hamlet. Thy state is the more gracious; for 'tis a vice to
know him. He hath much land, and fertile: let a beast be
lord of beasts, and his crib shall stand at the King's mess. 'Tis a
chough,[2] but, as I say, spacious in the possession of dirt.[3]

Osric. Sweet lord, if your lordship were at leisure, I should
impart a thing to you from his Majesty.

Hamlet. I will receive it, sir, with all diligence of spirit. Put
your bonnet to his right use; 'tis for the head.

Osric. I thank your lordship, it is very hot.

Hamlet. No, believe me, 'tis very cold: the wind is northerly.

Osric. It is indifferent cold,[4] my lord, indeed.

Hamlet. But yet methinks it is very sultry and hot for my
complexion.[5]

Osric. Exceedingly, my lord; it is very sultry, — as 'twere, —
I cannot tell how. But, my lord, his Majesty bade me signify to
you that he has laid a great wager on your head. Sir, this is the
matter, —

Hamlet. I beseech you, remember —

　　　　　　　　　　　[*Hamlet moves him to put on his hat.*

Osric. Nay, good my lord; for mine ease, in good faith. Sir,
here is newly come to court Laertes; believe me, an absolute
gentleman, full of most excellent differences,[6] of very soft society

---

[1] Ostentation.　　　　　　[2] Jackdaw.

[3] " Spacious in the possession of dirt," i.e., a large landowner.

[4] " Indifferent cold," i.e., somewhat cold.

[5] See Note 9, p. 42.

[6] " Excellent differences," i.e., distinguishing excellences.

and great showing: indeed, to speak feelingly of him, he is the card or calendar of gentry,[1] for you shall find in him the continent of what part a gentleman would see.

Hamlet. Sir, his definement suffers no perdition in you; though, I know, to divide him inventorially would dizzy the arithmetic of memory, and yet but yaw neither, in respect of his quick sail. But, in the verity of extolment, I take him to be a soul of great article; and his infusion of such dearth and rareness, as, to make true diction of him, his semblable is his mirror; and who else would trace him, his umbrage, nothing more.[2]

Osric. Your lordship speaks most infallibly of him.

Hamlet. The concernancy, sir? why do we wrap the gentleman in our more rawer breath?[3]

Osric. Sir?

Horatio. Is't not possible to understand in another tongue? You will do't, sir, really.

Hamlet. What imports the nomination of this gentleman?

Osric. Of Laertes?

Horatio. His purse is empty already; all's golden words are spent.

Hamlet. Of him, sir.

Osric. I know you are not ignorant —

Hamlet. I would you did, sir; yet, in faith, if you did, it would not much approve me.   Well, sir?

1 "The card or calendar of gentry," i.e., a perfect model of all gentlemanly accomplishments.

2 Warburton, in a note in Steevens and Johnson's Shakespeare (edition 1785), remarks on this passage: "It is designed as a specimen and ridicule of the court jargon of his [Shakespeare's] time. The sense in English is: 'He suffers nothing in your account of him, though to enumerate his good qualities particularly would be endless; yet when we have done our best, it would still come short of him. However, in strictness of truth, he is a great genius, and of a character so rarely to be met with, that, to find anything like him, we must look into his mirror, and his imitators will appear no more than his shadows.'"

3 "The concernancy," etc., i.e., why is it that you have brought this gentleman's name and excellences into our conversation?

Osric. You are not ignorant of what excellence Laertes is —

Hamlet. I dare not confess that, lest I should compare with him in excellence; but to know a man well were to know himself.

Osric. I mean, sir, for his weapon; but in the imputation laid on him by them, in his meed he's unfellow'd.

Hamlet. What's his weapon?

Osric. Rapier and dagger.

Hamlet. That's two of his weapons; but, well.

Osric. The King, sir, hath wager'd with him six Barbary horses; against the which he has impon'd,[1] as I take it, six French rapiers and poniards, with their assigns,[2] as girdle, hangers, and so. Three of the carriages, in faith, are very dear to fancy, very responsive to the hilts, most delicate carriages, and of very liberal conceit.[3]

Hamlet. What call you the carriages?

Horatio. I knew you must be edified by the margent[4] ere you had done.

Osric. The carriages, sir, are the hangers.

Hamlet. The phrase would be more germane[5] to the matter if we could carry cannon by our sides: I would it might be hangers till then. But, on: six Barbary horses against six French swords, their assigns, and three liberal-conceited carriages; that's the French bet against the Danish. Why is this "impon'd," as you call it?

Osric. The King, sir, hath laid, that, in a dozen passes between yourself and him, he shall not exceed you three hits: he hath laid on twelve for nine; and it would come to immediate trial, if your lordship would vouchsafe the answer.

Hamlet. How if I answer "no"?

---

[1] Wagered.   [2] Belongings; accompaniments.

[3] "Dear to fancy," etc., i.e., in excellent taste, harmonizing well with the hilts, and elaborately designed.

[4] "Edified by the margent," i.e., would require explanation of Osric's language.   [5] Relative.

Osric. I mean, my lord, the opposition of your person in trial.

Hamlet. Sir, I will walk here in the hall : if it please his Majesty, 'tis the breathing time of day with me ;[1] let the foils be brought, the gentleman willing, and the King hold his purpose, I will win for him an[2] I can ; if not, I will gain nothing but my shame and the odd hits.

Osric. Shall I redeliver you e'en so ?

Hamlet. To this effect, sir ; after what flourish your nature will.

Osric. I commend my duty to your lordship.

Hamlet. Yours, yours. [*Exit Osric.*] He does well to commend it himself ; there are no tongues else for's turn.

Horatio. This lapwing runs away with the shell on his head.[3]

Hamlet. He did comply with his dug,[4] before he suck'd it. Thus has he — and many more of the same bevy that I know the drossy age dotes on — only got the tune of the time and outward habit of encounter ;[5] a kind of yesty collection, which carries them through and through the most fond and winnowed opinions ; and do but blow them to their trial, the bubbles are out.

Enter a Lord.

Lord. My lord, his Majesty commended him to you by young Osric, who brings back to him that you attend him in the hall : he sends to know if your pleasure hold to play with Laertes, or that you will take longer time.

Hamlet. I am constant to my purposes ; they follow the King's pleasure : if his fitness speaks, mine is ready ; now, or whensoever, provided I be so able as now.

Lord. The King and Queen and all are coming down.

Hamlet. In happy time.

1 " Breathing time of day with me," i.e., my leisure, or resting time.

2 If.

3 " This lapwing runs," etc., i.e., this silly fellow, like the newly hatched lapwing, runs, etc.

4 " He did comply," etc., i.e., he formally begged pardon of the breast.

5 " The tune," etc., i.e., the fashionable manners and phrases of the time.

Lord. The Queen desires you to use some gentle entertainment to Laertes before you fall to play.

Hamlet. She well instructs me.   [*Exit Lord.*

Horatio. You will lose this wager, my lord.

Hamlet. I do not think so: since he went into France, I have been in continual practice; I shall win at the odds. But thou wouldst not think how ill all's here about my heart; but it is no matter.

Horatio. Nay, good my lord, —

Hamlet. It is but foolery; but it is such a kind of gaingiving[1] as would perhaps trouble a woman.

Horatio. If your mind dislike anything, obey it: I will forestall their repair hither, and say you are not fit.

Hamlet. Not a whit; we defy augury: there's a special providence in the fall of a sparrow. If it be now, 'tis not to come; if it be not to come, it will be now; if it be not now, yet it will come: the readiness is all. Since no man has aught of what he leaves, what is't to leave betimes?

Enter KING, QUEEN, LAERTES, Lords, OSRIC, *and* Attendants *with foils, etc.*

King. Come, Hamlet, come, and take this hand from me.
                    [*The King puts Laertes' hand into Hamlet's.*

Hamlet. Give me your pardon, sir: I've done you wrong;
But pardon't, as you are a gentleman.
This presence knows,
And you must needs have heard, how I am punish'd
With sore distraction. What I have done
That might your nature, honor, and exception[2]
Roughly awake, I here proclaim was madness.
Was't Hamlet wrong'd Laertes? Never Hamlet:
If Hamlet from himself be ta'en away,
And when he's not himself does wrong Laertes,

---

[1] Misgiving.
[2] In the sense of "take exception to," i.e., dislike.

Then Hamlet does it not, Hamlet denies it.
Who does it, then? His madness. If't be so,
Hamlet is of the faction that is wrong'd;
His madness is poor Hamlet's enemy.
Sir, in this audience,
Let my disclaiming from a purpos'd evil
Free me so far in your most generous thoughts,
That I have shot mine arrow o'er the house,
And hurt my brother.

Laertes.   I am satisfied in nature,
Whose motive, in this case, should stir me most
To my revenge; but in my terms of honor
I stand aloof, and will no reconcilement,
Till by some elder masters, of known honor,
I have a voice and precedent of peace,
To keep my name ungor'd.[1] But till that time
I do receive your offer'd love like love,
And will not wrong it.

Hamlet.   I embrace it freely,
And will this brother's wager frankly play.—
Give us the foils.— Come on.

Laertes.   •   Come, one for me.

Hamlet. I'll be your foil, Laertes: in mine ignorance
Your skill shall, like a star i' the darkest night,
Stick fiery off indeed.[2]

Laertes.   You mock me, sir.

Hamlet. No, by this hand.

King. Give them the foils, young Osric.— Cousin Hamlet,
You know the wager?

Hamlet.   Very well, my lord;
Your Grace hath laid the odds o' the weaker side.

King. I do not fear it; I have seen you both:
But since he is better'd, we have therefore odds.

[1] Unstained.
[2] " Stick fiery off indeed," i.e., appear more lustrous from the contrast.

Laertes. This is too heavy, let me see another.

Hamlet. This likes me well.[1]   These foils have all a length ?

[They prepare to play.

Osric. Ay, my good lord.

King. Set me the stoups of wine upon that table.
If Hamlet give the first or second hit,
Or quit in answer[2] of the third exchange,
Let all the battlements their ordnance fire;
The King shall drink to Hamlet's better breath;
And in the cup an union[3] shall he throw,
Richer than that which four successive kings
In Denmark's crown have worn.   Give me the cups;
And let the kettle[4] to the trumpet speak,
The trumpet to the cannoneer without,
The cannons to the heavens, the heavens to earth,
" Now the King drinks to Hamlet."— Come, begin.—
And you, the judges, bear a wary eye.[5]

Hamlet. Come on, sir.

Laertes.   Come, my lord.   *[They play.*

Hamlet.   One.

Laertes.   No.

Hamlet.   Judgment.

Osric. A hit, a very palpable hit.

Laertes.   Well; again.

King. Stay; give me drink.— Hamlet, this pearl is thine;
Here's to thy health.—

[Trumpets sound, and cannon shot off within.
Give him the cup.

Hamlet. I'll play this bout first; set it by a while.—
Come.   *[They play.]*   Another hit; what say you ?

---

[1] " This likes me well," i.e., I like this well.

[2] " Quit in answer," i.e., deliver a hit in retaliation.

[3] A pearl of the finest and most valuable kind was so called.

[4] Kettledrum.

[5] " Bear a wary eye," i.e., watch the playing closely.

Laertes. A touch, a touch, I do confess.

King. Our son shall win.

Queen.   He's fat, and scant of breath.—
Here, Hamlet, take my napkin, rub thy brows:
The Queen carouses[1] to thy fortune, Hamlet.

Hamlet. Good madam !

King.   Gertrude, do not drink.

Queen. I will, my lord : I pray you, pardon me.

King. [*Aside*] It is the poison'd cup : it is too late.

Hamlet. I dare not drink yet, madam ; by and by.

Queen. Come, let me wipe thy face.

Laertes. My lord, I'll hit him now.

King.   I do not think't.

Laertes. [*Aside*] And yet 'tis almost 'gainst my conscience.

Hamlet. Come, for the third, Laertes.   You but dally ;
I pray you, pass with your best violence.
I am afeard you make a wanton of me.[2]

Laertes. Say you so ? come on.   [*They play.*

Osric. Nothing, neither way.

Laertes. Have at you now !

> [*Laertes wounds Hamlet; then, in scuffling, they
> change rapiers, and Hamlet wounds Laertes.*

King.   Part them ; they are incens'd.

Hamlet. Nay, come, again.   [*The Queen falls.*

Osric.   Look to the Queen there, ho !

Horatio. They bleed on both sides.— How is it, my lord ?

Osric. How is't, Laertes ?

Laertes. Why, as a woodcock to mine own springe,[3] Osric ;
I am justly kill'd with mine own treachery.

Hamlet. How does the Queen?

King.   She swoons to see them bleed.

Queen. No, no, the drink, the drink,— O my dear Hamlet !—
The drink, the drink !   I am poison'd.   [*Dies.*

---

[1] Drinks.   [2] " Make a wanton of me," i.e., trifle as with a child.
[3] See Note 4, p. 40.

Hamlet. O villainy! Ho! let the door be lock'd. Treachery!
Seek it out.

Laertes. It is here, Hamlet. Hamlet, thou art slain;
No medicine in the world can do thee good;
In thee there is not half an hour of life:
The treacherous instrument is in thy hand,
Unbated and envenom'd. The foul practice [1]
Hath turn'd itself on me; lo, here I lie,
Never to rise again. Thy mother's poison'd;
I can no more. The King, the King's to blame.

Hamlet. The point envenom'd too!
Then, venom, to thy work.   [*Stabs the King.*

All. Treason! treason!

King. O, yet defend me, friends; I am but hurt.

Hamlet. Here, thou incestuous, murd'rous, damned Dane,
Drink off this potion. Is thy union here?
Follow my mother.   [*King dies.*

Laertes.   He is justly serv'd;
It is a poison temper'd [2] by himself.
Exchange forgiveness with me, noble Hamlet:
Mine and my father's death come not upon thee,
Nor thine on me!   [*Dies.*

Hamlet. Heaven make thee free of it! I follow thee. —
I am dead, Horatio. — Wretched Queen, adieu! —
You that look pale and tremble at this chance,[3]
That are but mutes or audience to this act,
Had I but time, — as this fell sergeant, death,
Is strict in his arrest, — O, I could tell you —
But let it be. — Horatio, I am dead;
Thou liv'st: report me and my cause aright
To the unsatisfied.

Horatio.   Never believe it:

[1] "Foul practice," i.e., iniquitous plot.
[2] Prepared.
[3] Mischance.

I am more an an'tique Roman than a Dane.
Here's yet some liquor left.

    Hamlet.   As thou'rt a man,
Give me the cup: let go; by Heaven, I'll have't.
O good Horatio, what a wounded name,
Things standing thus unknown, shall live behind me!
If thou didst ever hold me in thy heart,
Absent thee from felicity a while,
And in this harsh world draw thy breath in pain,
To tell my story.   [*March afar off, and shot within*
               What warlike noise is this?

    Osric.   Young Fortinbras, with conquest[1] come from Poland,
To th' ambassadors of England gives
This warlike volley.

    Hamlet.   O, I die, Horatio;
The potent poison quite o'ercrows[2] my spirit:
I cannot live to hear the news from England;
But I do prophesy the election lights
On Fortinbras: he has my dying voice;
So tell him, with the occurrents,[3] more and less,
Which have solicited.[4]   The rest is silence.   [*Dies.*

    Horatio.   Now cracks a noble heart.   Good night, sweet prince;
And flights of angels sing thee to thy rest!—
Why does the drum come hither?   [*March within.*

      Enter FORTINBRAS, *the* English Ambassadors, *and* others.

    Fortinbras.   Where is this sight?

    Horatio.   What is it ye would see?
If aught of woe or wonder, cease your search.

    Fortinbras.   This quarry[5] cries on[6] havoc.[7]   O proud death,

---

[1] "With conquest," i.e., victorious.   [2] Triumphs over.
[3] Occurrences.   [4] Brought on the event.
[5] Pile of dead game; a hunting term.   [6] "Cries on," i.e., indicates.
[7] "Havoc!" was the cry in battle when no quarter was to be given;
hence, indiscriminate slaughter.

What feast is toward in thine eternal cell,
That thou so many princes at a shot
So bloodily hast struck?

   First Ambassador.   The sight is dismal;
And our affairs from England come too late:
The ears are senseless that should give us hearing,
To tell him his commandment is fulfill'd,
That Rosencrantz and Guildenstern are dead.
Where should we have our thanks?

   Horatio.   Not from his mouth,
Had it the ability of life to thank you:
He never gave commandment for their death.
But since, so jump upon this bloody question,[1]
You from the Polack wars, and you from England,
Are here arriv'd, give order that these bodies
High on a stage be placed to the view;
And let me speak to the yet unknowing world
How these things came about: so shall you hear
Of carnal, bloody, and unnatural acts,
Of accidental judgments, casual slaughters,
Of deaths put on by cunning and forc'd cause,
And, in this upshot, purposes mistook,
Fall'n on the inventors' heads: all this can I
Truly deliver.

   Fortinbras.   Let us haste to hear it,
And call the noblest to the audience.
For me, with sorrow I embrace my fortune:
I have some rights of memory in this kingdom,
Which now to claim my vantage doth invite me.[2]

   Horatio. Of that I shall have also cause to speak,
And from his mouth whose voice will draw no more:

---

[1] "Jump upon this bloody question," i.e., just at the moment of these bloody events.

[2] "Some rights," etc., i.e., some rights in this kingdom that are remembered, and which opportunity invites me to claim.

But let this same be presently perform'd,
Even while men's minds are wild; lest more mischance,
On plots and errors, happen.

 Fortinbras.   Let four captains
Bear Hamlet, like a soldier, to the stage;
For he was likely, had he been put on,
To have prov'd most royally; [1] and, for his passage,
The soldiers' music and the rites of war
Speak loudly for him.
Take up the bodies. Such a sight as this
Becomes the field, but here shows much amiss.
Go, bid the soldiers shoot.

     [*A dead march. Exeunt, bearing off the dead bodies;
       after which a peal of ordnance is shot off.*

---

[1] " For he was likely," etc., i.e., for, if he had succeeded to the throne, it is likely he would have proved a most worthy sovereign.

THE ELIZABETHAN THEATER.

In order to understand and appreciate thoroughly the purpose of the scenes in *Hamlet*, one should know something about the mechanical structure of a Shakespearean play; but as this mechanical structure depended largely upon the mechanical structure of the Elizabethan stage, one should first know something about that.

The theaters of Queen Elizabeth's time were divided into two classes, public and private. Both were practically alike in structure, [1] except that the private theater was roofed—the public theater proper had no covering; only the stage was roofed. The best type of private theater was "Blackfriars," erected by a noble for the entertainment of his aristocratic friends only. We shall take for illustrative purposes, however, the Globe Theater, erected in 1614 on the site of the original Globe which burned down during a performance of *Henry VIII*. The new Globe was the highest and best type of public theater.

The Globe Theater was octagonal in shape. Its stone walls were perforated here and there by small windows. From the outside two superstructures could be seen projecting above the walls. These superstructures supported a third, which was topped by a flagstaff. Inside the general structure was practically the same as it is to-day, except for the stage. The diagram on page 166 will help explain the salient features of the Elizabethan stage.

[1] The following details, however, should be noted: in the public theater, admission was by payment; there were no tickets used; both common people and aristocrats were admitted; there were no seats in the pit; performances took place only in the daytime (3 o'clock in the afternoon). In the private theater admission was by invitation; only aristocrats were admitted; there were no seats in the parterre, or pit as it was called in the public theater; and lastly, performances took place, not only in the daytime (3 o'clock in the afternoon), but also at night. Candles and torches were used for illumination.

It consisted of three parts: the front,[1] which projected way out into the pit;[2] the middle, separated from the front by a large curtain hung between two stout pillars; and the rear stage (which was practically a balcony), supported by two posts and screened from the audience when not in use by another curtain. Between these posts was a third curtain, which separated the middle stage from the "tiring room."[3] Above the middle stage was a small room called the "heavens." It contained machinery for letting down heavy properties. On the floor of this stage were trapdoors through which demons descended. These doors were

Sketch of the Stage of the Globe Theater, London, erected 1614.

[1] This part of the stage was not roofed.

[2] Corresponds to our parquet. Here the "groundlings" stood—there were no seats.

[3] Actor's dressing room.

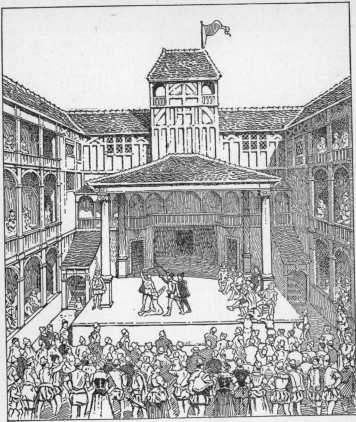

Interior of the Fortune Theater, London, erected in 1599.

(Note that the plan of the stage differs but slightly from that of the Globe Theater.)

used effectively in grave scenes (See *Hamlet*, Act V). Authorities differ as to the use of space above the tiring room. (Referred to above as "rear stage.") Some say that it was used as a balcony for spectators,[1] but it is not likely that Elizabethan audiences cared

---

[1] De Witt's drawing of the interior of the Swan Theater, made about 1596, supports this view. Here we see that the balcony is apparently a continuation of the first gallery.

to view the backs of the actors: besides, from such a position they would not be able to hear. This balcony, or rear stage, was used, no doubt, for stage kings and their courts, for Roman emperors viewing a scene in the arena, or to represent the tops of city walls. Here, for instance, Richard of Gloucester in *Richard III* made his hypocritical appeal to the people, supported by two churchmen. Here, also, Juliet stood in the famous "balcony scene." Above the rear stage was another small room, corresponding to our "fly gallery." Here scenery, such as a painted curtain for the rear of this stage, was kept. This painted curtain corresponds to our "back drop." The two superstructures mentioned above were simply the tops or roofs of this gallery and the "heavens."

Possibly we have wondered at the multiplicity of scenes in a Shakespearean play and how these scenes were arranged without confusion. As we shall soon see, there was no confusion at all. Shakespeare could present all of his scenes harmoniously and effectively because he had practically a four-part stage.[1] He could begin his performance by giving the dramatic exposition on the front stage, and then he could use the other stages for the further interpretation of the play. He could not only harmoniously and effectively present these scenes to the public one after the other, but he could also present them simultaneously.[2] (Note the resemblance to the modern three-ringed circus!) In this way he could show more vividly the connection between scenes. Let us take to illustrate this connection scenes from *Romeo and Juliet*. The curtain parts in the middle and an ivy-crowned performer steps out and recites the prologue. As soon as he retires, two stout youths spring upon the front stage and rant in high-pitched voices; others follow—rival parties encounter each other—finally the lords of the rival houses of Montague and Capulet appear upon the scene and Shakespeare's romantic masterpiece is flashed before the audience. With what tense and eager faces must the Elizabethan playgoers have followed the action of the drama, laugh-

[1] Including the tiring room that could be used to represent a tomb or a bedchamber.

[2] Professor Brandl says that the three separate divisions of the Elizabethan stage were sometimes all in use together, that three different groups of persons could in some measure claim the attention of the audience at the same time.

ing at the wit of Mercutio, greeting with ribald merriment that oddly assorted pair, Peter and the Nurse, cursing Tybalt, and finally sobbing at the tragic dénouement in the tomb! To be more specific, in Act II, Scene 3, how keenly the irony of fate is shown if the audience can turn instantly from watching Romeo's banishment below, to Juliet above, waiting for his coming with impatient joy and rapture. Again, in the reception hall of Act IV, Scene 4, (middle stage) they can see Lady Capulet, the nurse, and servants preparing the wedding banquet. Pretty soon the nurse goes upstairs into the balcony [1] (rear stage) and tries to awaken the sleeping Juliet. She draws back the curtains, but she cannot arouse the sleeper, and frightened, calls for help. Then are heard the cries of lamentation and despair as the scene is changed from a wedding to a funeral. In the midst of the tumult the musicians begin playing on the front stage totally oblivious to the tragedy enacted behind their backs. In conclusion let us take a few brief examples from other plays. In *Julius Cæsar* when Brutus and Antony go into the pulpit, they simply mount into the rear balcony. In Act IV the front stage represents the ground in front of Brutus' tent; the quarrel scene takes place on the middle stage which represents the interior of the tent of Brutus. In *King John* when Arthur kills himself by jumping from the city walls, he falls from the rear balcony, and so on. How vividly were these scenes presented to the audience of Shakespeare's day! No wonder that to-day we cannot present the plays of the great dramatist in a more effective way. With our one-part stage we cannot thoroughly appreciate the nice distinctions between scenes and acts. Scenes are to-day united that Shakespeare kept apart; the order of the parts of the play is frequently ignored and many passages and even whole scenes are omitted altogether, as for example the scene introducing the musicians in Act IV of *Romeo and Juliet*. Long waits between the acts make it necessary to mutilate the play in many ways. If we used the three-part stage we could shorten the time it takes to present a Shakespearean play, by eliminating the delay between acts and scenes.

Realizing the limitations of the modern stage from a Shakespearean standpoint, some enterprising managers are using the revolving stage

[1] Tiring room could not, of course, be effectively used here for a bedchamber.

invented by Herr Lautenschlaeger of Munich in 1901. Dr. von Possart, director of the Munich Court Theater, declared at the time of the invention that this type of stage promised to be "the stage of the future." This worthy invention seems to solve the problem of presenting the five-act drama, with its multiplicity of scenes, in a thoroughly satisfactory manner.[1]

NOTES AND QUESTIONS ON HAMLET.

I. MASTERY OF THE PLOT.

In studying a literary work of any kind, the student should first gain a knowledge of the plot as a whole. This he can do at a single sitting outside of the classroom. He should not refer to the notes or glossary. After he has thus obtained a reasonably sound knowledge of the plot, he is ready to make a more detailed study of the masterpiece under the direction of the teacher.

II. CLASSIFICATION.

Shakespeare's plays are divided into two classes, Tragedy and Comedy. Comedy may be subdivided as follows: Tragi-Comedy, Romantic Comedy, Pure Comedy, and Farce.

A Tragedy is a dramatic representation of serious, complete and unified action having a fatal ending.

A Tragi-Comedy is a drama in which the plot works up to a crisis where the guilty one must face his own deed. He has a chance to repent; if he do so, the threatened tragedy is turned to a comedy. If he do not repent, however, the evildoer goes willfully deeper and deeper into crime and the play is of course a tragedy.

A Romantic Comedy is a drama in which the main action is on the whole dignified and serious. The humorous element is prominent in connection with subcharacters or in subactions. The *main action* contains adventure and romantic love as points of interest.

Pure Comedy is a drama in which the central and perhaps the only action is filled with humor.

[1] The revolving stage is not entirely new, for the Japanese have used it for a very long period, according to Dr. Iyenaga.

Farce is a drama which contains improbable or absurd situations in order to excite laughter and action.

To which class does *Hamlet* belong?

Give examples of the above mentioned classes.

III. PLOT.

Plots may be simple or complex. The simple plot deals with one character or a single group of characters and follows their fortunes to the end. The complex plot contains several groups; it has a main story or action and one or more rival or secondary stories, or sub-actions. In other words, if the plot is not one story, but several stories told side by side, it is called complex. The *Merchant of Venice* has a complex plot, for it has a main action, that of the pound of flesh, and a subaction, the elopement of Jessica.

Is the plot of *Hamlet* simple or complex?

If complex, how many separate stories has it?

Give examples of plays containing simple and complex plots.

Source of Plot.—Shakespeare took the subject matter for his Greek and Roman plays from Plutarch's *Lives*, translated by North; his English and historical plays he took largely from Holinshed's *Chronicle.*[1] The plots of other plays are taken from classical writers, such as Plautus, or Italian writers, as Ariosto (1474–1533).

Did Shakespeare borrow his plots and enlarge upon them, or did he evolve the plots himself? What was his practice in this respect?

Was Shakespeare gifted with much originality?

To what extent do you find the story of *Hamlet* different from the original? [2]

IV. SETTING.

What is the historical period in which the play is supposed to occur?

How much time does the action of the play cover? See Act I, Scene 2 and Act III, Scene 2.

Where is the scene of the action laid?

---

[1] Both books can be obtained. Morley's edition of the plays, in Cassell's National Library, gives ample information regarding the source of each play.

[2] This may form the subject for a theme.

Is it real or imaginary?

Is there little or much description of place? Quote lines.

Does the author introduce local color; that is, objects, customs, expressions, or details of dress peculiar to the place described?

V. CHARACTERS.

Make a study of the principal characters. Take up each character and follow him through the play and note his development or nondevelopment by what he says and does. A character is developing when the experiences he undergoes change him so that he is more generous, more cruel, or more serious, etc., than at the beginning of the play. A character is nondeveloping when in spite of experience his nature remains the same.

Is Hamlet a developing or nondeveloping character?

What group of characters are associated with him?

What characters group themselves against him? Who is the central figure of the opposing group?

Do any characters serve as connecting links between the two groups? If they do, they help give unity to the plot.

Are the characters clearly distinguished? What can you say of Rosencrantz and Guildenstern as characters?

Is Polonius a humorous character? How does his humor differ from that of the First Gravedigger?

On the whole is there *marked* character development in the play?

What can you say of the duration of action? Has the time scheme (length or brevity) anything to do with character development? What?

Hamlet's Character.—What does his first speech reveal of his character? What does the Queen's reply reveal of it? His soliloquy?

How is his morality and refinement shown here?

Does he show traces of a suspicious nature when he greets Horatio?

What lines show a philosophic trend of mind?

Where does he show that he lacks steadfastness of purpose?

A noted author once said, "Hamlet is Germany"—can you see the resemblance?

In what way does Hamlet resemble Brutus in *Julius Cæsar* and Jaques in *As You Like It?*

How are Brutus and Hamlet disqualified for action? (See Introduction.)

What lines ought to dispel for all time questions as to Hamlet's sanity?

Is Hamlet's description of Horatio's character in Act III a help in this respect?

VI. Structure.

(*Mechanical.*)

The various steps in the development of the plot give rise to a division into acts and scenes. A Shakespearean play consists of five acts; the number of scenes varies. These acts have been described respectively by the following terms: Exposition, Ascending Action, Climax, Descending Action, and Conclusion.

Act I (*Exposition.*)

1. The situation is outlined.
2. The chief characters are introduced.
3. The keynote of each character is given.
4. The main action is begun.

Act II (*Ascending Action.*)

1. The plot begins to develop.
2. Characters are more clearly rounded out.
3. Motives are made known.
4. New characters are sometimes introduced.

Act III (*Climax.*)

1. Turning point is reached.
2. The guilty one still has a chance to repent. If he do so, the threatened Tragedy is turned to Comedy. If he do not repent, however, he must go on to the end and suffer the consequences of his misdeeds. Then the play is a Tragedy.

Act IV (*Descending Action.*)

1. This act works out the consequences of the result of the guilty one's decision in Act III.

2. New characters are often introduced—sometimes to take the places of others. In Tragedy the guilty one plunges still deeper into crime.

Act V (Conclusion.)

1. Forces become reconciled. The discordant element is destroyed. Harmony is restored either through destruction of the criminal (cf. King Richard in *Richard III*), as in Tragedy, or through conformity to ethical laws, as in Comedy.

VII. STRUCTURE.

(Dramatic.)

Let us now see how mechanical and dramatic structure go hand in hand.

Act I (Exposition.)

The first four scenes are preparatory. Scenes 1 and 4 especially arouse our interest. Can you see how?

Scene 2 gives us the situation in Denmark—in particular the relation of Hamlet to the King and Queen.

Scene 3 gives Hamlet's relations to Ophelia.

The keynotes of the principal characters are struck—Hamlet in Scenes 2 and 5, and Ophelia in Scene 3. What can you say of the characters so far?

Scene 5 begins the main action of the play. What is it?

To sum up, in Act I Shakespeare has shown us the causes for action. Where has he clearly foreshadowed that action? He has introduced all the principal characters and outlined their traits. He has made the emotional chord vibrate. He has created local color and dramatic atmosphere.

Act II (Ascending Action.)

How is the action advanced slightly in Scene 1?

How is the main action advanced in Scene 2?

What preparation is there in this scene for Scene 1 of Act III?

The characters of Hamlet and Ophelia are further developed in Scene 1. In Scene 2 we see a further development of Hamlet's character in his long soliloquy. A subaction in this scene is the employment of Guildenstern and Rosencrantz to spy upon Hamlet.

Hamlet wishes to accomplish the death of the King, his uncle—his motive is to avenge his father's murder. He is opposed by his weaker self—his fatal tendency to think and dream instead of act.

What new characters are introduced?

Act III (Climax.)

Scene 1 carries forward the main action, for here the King consents to see the play.

He betrays his guilt in Scene 2. He will not repent, however, (III, 3) so the play is a Tragedy.

The climax is in Act III, Scene 2 where Hamlet is convinced of the King's guilt.

The turning point is in Scene 3, where Hamlet lets go the opportunity to kill the King. What trait of character is here shown?

Hamlet's character is further shown in Scene 2 in his talk with Horatio and others.

Scene 4 is a scene of action. What is accomplished?

Act IV (Descending Action.)

The descending action is apparent at the close of Act III, Scene 4, where Hamlet seems willing to go to England.

Does he thus appear to forget all about his revenge?

What new character is introduced? Why did Shakespeare get rid of Polonius?

How do Scenes 1, 2, and 3 advance a subaction—the sending away of Hamlet to England?

Scene 5 deals with a subaction,—the madness of Ophelia and Laertes' rebellion. Both are results of what act and scene?

How do Scenes 4, 6, and 7 each advance the main action?

The guilty one, the King, plunges deeper into crime, for in Scene 7 he and Laertes plan the death of Hamlet.

Act V (Conclusion.)

What contrast is introduced in Scene 1? How is the main action here advanced? How is it still further advanced in Scene 2? In this scene the tragic element is supreme, for the Queen, King, Laertes, and Hamlet are killed. The guilty one, the King, is destroyed and harmony is restored in the person of Fortinbras.

VIII. Contrast.

Shakespeare understood well the power of contrast, and used this device effectively. Contrast is absolutely necessary in Hamlet to relieve the mental strain on the audience. Too much bloodshed has a depressing effect, so the dramatist brightened his play by a change in mood.

Contrast may be in the plot, as where a defeat is followed by a victory, or vice versa; or it may be in mood or tone, as when comedy follows pathos; or it may be in character, two persons being introduced who are opposites; again, there may be a contrast between the same person's actions on separate occasions. Note, for example, the contrast in character of Sir Launfal in Lowell's *Vision of Sir Launfal* before and after the dream. There may be contrast in description also.

Closely allied to contrast is parallelism, or the introduction of similar characters and incidents. To illustrate, in *As You Like It* the characters in the subactions fall in love in the same manner that the characters in the main action do—it is a case of "love at first sight" in each case.

Point out examples of contrast in *Hamlet*.

Point out examples of parallelism, either in character or incident.

Outside Reading.

For a brief biography of Shakespeare read Dowden's *Primer*, Chap. II (Amer. Bk. Co.), or Wendell's *William Shakspere*, Chap. II (Scribner's). For a more complete treatment, however, see Sydney Lee's *Life* (Macmillan). Hamilton Wright Mabie has written a delightful history of the great dramatist.

For manners and customs, particularly theatrical, read Geo. Brandes' *William Shakespeare, A Critical Study*, Chaps. 1 to 4; also the first two chapters of Dowden's *Primer*.

Recent magazine material: "A Daring Reconstruction of Shakespeare's Personality from his Plays," by Frank Harris, in *Current Literature* for Dec., 1909. "New Shakespeare Discoveries" in *Harper's Magazine*, Mar., 1910, by C. W. Wallace, Ph. D., University of Nebraska, contains some interesting material regarding Shakespeare's London life, of which so little is known.

"Frailty thy name is woman"
          Hamlet.

"Till then sit still, my soul: foul deeds will
          rise,
though all the earth o'erwhelm them, to men's
          eyes." Hamlet

The time is out of joint: O cursed spite,
That ever I was born to set it right.
          Hamlet

Brevity is the soul of wit
          Polonius

Though this be madness, yet there is
method in it. Polonius

Rich gifts wax poor when givers
prove unkind.
          Ophelia

Sweets to the sweet
          Queen

There's a divinity that shapes our ends
          Hamlet.